Distant Horizons
From Midwest to Middle East

Mike Trial

Published by AKA-Publishing
Columbia, Missouri 65203
www.aka-publishing.com

ISBN 978-1-936688-57-9

Distant Horizons

From Midwest to Middle East

Mike Trial

For Linden
1950-2012

The Trial Family

John (Mack) Wallace
Born: April 18, 1860 Warren County, Illinois
Died: February 17, 1950 Kansas City, Missouri

Juniata (Juna) Alianore Porter
Born: February 4, 1879, Vernon County, Missouri
Died: July 30, 1957 Kansas City, Missouri

Lloyd Trial
Born: April 27, 1884 Muscotah, Kansas
Died: December 22, 1933 Muscotah, Kansas

Grace Talbert
Born: July 12, 1888 Willis, Kansas
Died: September 16, 1973 Holton, Kansas

Married May 4, 1904 Vernon County, Missouri

Married February 16, 1907

Bonnie Louisa Wallace
Born: February 10, 1905 Kansas City, Missouri
Died: May 2, 1959 Kansas City, Missouri

Juniata Ruth Wallace
Born: July 24, 1912 Nevada, Missouri
Died: June 13, 1969 Columbia, Missouri

George Talbert Trial
Born: December 1, 1910 Muscotah, Kansas
Died: December 13, 1996 Columbia, Missouri

Married: May 20, 1940 Kansas City, Missouri

Doris Gilmore
Born: York, Nebraska
Died: Superior, Wisconsin

John (Jack) Porter Wallace
Born: May 8, 1909 Kansas City, Missouri
Died: October 6, 1988 Superior, Wisconsin

Michael George Trial
Born: September 14, 1946 Kansas City, Missouri

Linden Trial
Born: June 21, 1950 Kansas City, Missouri
Died: June 10, 2012 Columbia Missouri

Married: November 25, 1947

John (Mack) Wallace

Born: April 18, 1860 Warren County, Illinois
Married: Juna Porter; May 4, 1904, Vernon County, Missouri
Died: February 17, 1950 Kansas City, Missouri

Juniata (Juna) Alianore Porter

Born: February 4, 1879, Vernon County, Missouri
Married: Mack Wallace; May 4, 1904, Vernon County, Missouri
Died: July 30, 1957, Kansas City, Missouri

Children born to Juna and Mack Wallace:

Bonnie Louisa Wallace

Born: February 10, 1905 Kansas City, Missouri
Died: May 2, 1959, Kansas City, Missouri

John (Jack) Porter Wallace

Born: May 8, 1909 Kansas City Missouri
Married: Doris Gilmore; November 25, 1947
Died: October 6, 1988 Superior, Wisconsin

Juniata Ruth Wallace

Born: July 24, 1912, Nevada, Missouri
Married: George Trial; May 20, 1940 Kansas City, Missouri
Died: June 13, 1969 Columbia, Missouri

Trial Family Tree

Lloyd Trial
Born: April 27, 1884, Muscotah, Kansas
Married: Grace Talbert February 16, 1907
Died: December 22, 1933, Muscotah, Kansas

Grace Talbert
Born: July 12, 1888 Willis, Kansas
Married: Lloyd Trial; February 16, 1907
Died: September 16, 1973 Holton, Kansas

Child born to Lloyd and Grace Trial:

George Talbert Trial
Born: December 1, 1910 Muscotah, Kansas
Married: Ruth Wallace; May 20 1940, Kansas City, Missouri
Died: December 13, 1996 Columbia, Missouri

Children born to George and Ruth Trial:

Michael George Trial
Born: September 14, 1946 Kansas City, Missouri

Linden Trial
Born: June 21, 1950 Kansas City, Missouri
Died: June 10, 2012 Columbia, Missouri

Foreword

My father, George Trial, was born and raised on a farm in eastern Kansas. My mother, Ruth Wallace, grew up in Kansas City. They were both working as teachers in Kansas City when they met and married in 1940. I was born in Kansas City in 1946. After military service in World War II my father stayed on active duty with the Air Force and in 1948 was transferred to the tiny Air Force base at Dhahran, Saudi Arabia. In 1949 my mother took me, age three, to live with George at the airbase in Saudi Arabia. For the next year my parents and I traveled extensively in the Middle East, Ethiopia, India, and Thailand. In 1950 my mother and I returned to Kansas City where my sister Linden was born.

This book traces my parents' journey from the Midwest to the Middle East, and tells how that journey changed their lives.

Chapter 1

Sitting on the lawn in front of the house in the soft summer morning, Ruth was daydreaming. The breeze ruffled her straight brown hair. Her book lay face down beside her; in her mind's eye she sat in front of a castle and on the distant horizon a knight in armor was riding toward her.

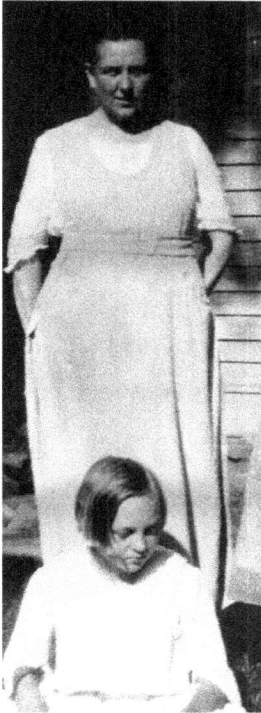

Ruth's mother Juna stood on the porch watching Ruth for a moment. Then she shook her head and let the screen door clack shut behind her. Ruth looked around. "I need your help in the garden," Juna called.

Ruth got up and went to help her mother tie up the tomato plants. But in her mind she continued the endlessly changing adventures of Launcelot, Guenevere, Tristan, Isolde, and the quest for the Grail. She pictured herself in those stories, adventuring across that misty landscape. She was a happy child, a bit of a dreamer. It was 1925 and she was thirteen years old. The Wallace family lived on a small farm near the tiny village of Sandstone in Vernon County, Missouri, one hundred miles south of Kansas City.

After the tomatoes were tied up, Ruth and her mother picked beans and carried the basket of beans up onto the porch to shell them. "Don't leave that library book lying out there," Juna told Ruth. She retrieved it and put it on the table. She'd take it back to the library after lunch today. Nevada, the county seat of Vernon County had quite a good library. A college too—Cottey College—which the town fathers were exceedingly proud of.

Mack and Juna had married in May 1904, and had moved into their first home, a two-story white frame house not far from Mack's father's farm. The house was fronted with a wide porch and four wooden pillars. The family kept rocking chairs on the front porch, perfect for sitting and chatting on long summer evenings, or reading in the cool shade of a summer afternoon while the breeze moved the clouds around the summer sky. The chirp of insects stirring in the grass and the sighing of dusty leaves in the big oak and elm trees back of the house were familiar daytime sounds. At night, the brilliant stars adorned the sky and Ruth often viewed them from her window as she lay on her bed.

CERTIFIED COPY OF

Marriage License

STATE OF MISSOURI, COUNTY OF ___VERNON___

This license authorizes any licensed or ordained Preacher of the Gospel, who is a Citizen of the United States, or who is a resident of this State and a Pastor of any church in this State, or by any Judge of a Court of Record, except Judges of the Probate Court, to solemnize Marriage between

___John M. Wallace___ of ___Kansas City___
in the County of ___Jackson___ and State of ___Missouri___
who is ___past___ the age of twenty-one years,
and ___Juniata A. Porter___
of ___Nevada___ in the County of ___Vernon___
and State of ___Missouri___ who is ___past___ the age of eighteen years

___(SEAL)___

WITNESS my hand as Recorder of Deeds with the Seal of Office hereto
(SEAL) affixed at my Office in ~~Nevada~~ this ___4"___
day of ___May___, 19 ___04___
By ___Young Ewing___ ___G. G. Ewing___
Deputy. Recorder of Deeds

STATE OF MISSOURI,
County of ___Vernon___ } ss. This is to Certify that the undersigned ___Minister of the Gospel___ did, at
___Nevada___ in said County, on the ___4"___
day of ___May___, A. D. 19 ___04___, unite in Marriage the above
named persons and I further Certify that I am legally qualified under the Laws of the State of Missouri to solemnize Marriages.
___G. D. Edwards___

The foregoing certificate of marriage was filed for record in my office on the ___5"___
day of ___May___ ~~19 04~~
___G. G. Ewing___ Recorder of Deeds
By ___Irene Gordon___ Deputy.

STATE OF MISSOURI,
County of ___Vernon___ } ss. I, ___Frank Marquardt___
Recorder of Deeds within and for the County of ___Vernon___, aforesaid, do hereby
certify that the above and foregoing is a full, true and complete copy of the above Marriage License as the same appears of record in my office.

IN TESTIMONY WHEREOF, I hereunto set my hand and affix the seal of
said office, at ___Nevada___, Missouri,
this ___2nd___ day of ___May___ A. D., 19 ___50___.
___Frank Marquardt___ Recorder.
By ___Irene Gordon___ Deputy

5

Ruth sometimes wandered the fields and woods across the pasture to a tiny creek where frogs jumped and blue jays squawked in the sycamores overhead. Once, when Ruth was four and Jack seven, they followed their older sister Louisa on explorations of the nearby fields. They'd returned across the pasture near milking

time. A cow stood in their path. Ruth and Jack were scared, but Louisa had the situation in hand. She fearlessly looked the cow in the face, then led them past.

As Ruth finished setting the table for lunch, she heard her father's car pull up. "How's everybody this fine summer day?" he said with a smile as he came inside.

Mack was a real estate agent. Ruth could tell from the way her mother and father skirted the subject that her grandparents had been disappointed when Mack decided to be a real estate man instead of a farmer. But he was quite successful in his real estate dealings, so Juna was pacified. Today he had news for the family.

"We're moving to town," Mack told them. "I closed the deal on the new house this morning. It's on Central Avenue, number 305." He smiled. "Just two blocks to Central Square," he gave his wife a meaningful look, "and Cottey College." Ruth knew her mother was adamant that Louisa go to Cottey College.

Mack Wallace owned one of the best cars in Vernon County. He'd often take Louisa with him on his buying and selling trips around the county. Sometimes Ruth would go with him to her grandparents' while Mack helped his father with the family farm. She'd watch them cutting and raking the hay in the field across the creek from their house from the shade of an oak tree while Mack ran the mule-drawn rake. It was pleasant to inhale the aroma of the fresh-cut hay that permeated the summer air.

Ruth was born in 1912, the youngest of three children. She was a shy girl, content to live in the shadow of her older brother Jack, who was a cheerful, gregarious child, and Louisa, her older sister.

As long as Ruth could remember, her older sister Louisa, who now wanted everyone to call her 'Bonnie', had been her parents' favorite—an intense and beautiful baby who became an intense and beautiful girl, the undisputed leader of the three kids. Bonnie was a smart, sociable, self-assured, and secretive girl with flashing brown eyes and waist-length brunette hair. Despite her protests, Juna had forced Bonnie to grow her hair long. But now that it was waist-length, Ruth thought her sister was inordinately proud of it. She missed no chance to be the center of attention when grown-ups were around.

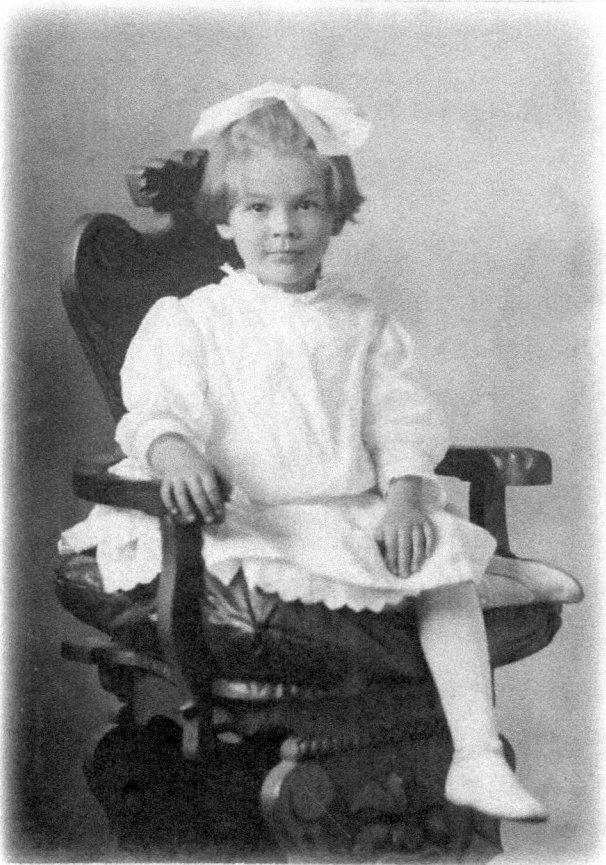

Juna put Bonnie in charge of watching Ruth and Jack, and Bonnie took the role seriously. She told Ruth and Jack

8

what games they'd play, where they'd go exploring, and the books they'd read. The kids went barefoot around the neighborhood, except when their mother caught them and made them put their shoes on. "You look like ragamuffins," she'd tell them.

Jack would often slip away to go about his own games, but Ruth always followed Bonnie. They'd trek across the fields to Miller's pond or down the creek to the trestle bridge where Highway 94 crossed the creek. As they walked the girls invented stories of distant places, imagining the hayfields were Avignon or Catalonia in the books their mother insisted they read. Juna also insisted the girls learn French, so they were tutored every Saturday morning at the home of Mrs. Colton, the French wife of the stationery store owner. Much to the girls' dismay, Mrs. Colton also found two short French novels suitable for use as reading practice. After practicing greetings, vocabulary and verbs for an hour, Bonnie and Ruth would trudge home, where Juna would make them sit in the rocking chairs on the front porch and read their books while she wrote letters. Jack sometimes joined them, grinning over his Edgar Rice Burroughs books. Frustrated at this obvious injustice, Bonnie faced her mother, dark eyes flashing. "It's not fair. Jack gets to read *Tarzan* books in English and we have to study French."

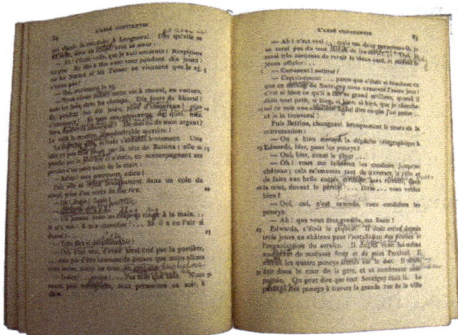

Juna was patient. "It's good for you to learn a little of another language."

Bonnie demanded, "Why?"

"Sit down and read," Juna said; her tone was final. But when Juna had bought Jack another book for his birthday, she had the girls write their names in it and pretend it was from them.

Juna maintained a small shelf of books in the parlor and a few more on the dresser in her bedroom. Books with titles like *Bardelys the Magnificent*, *A Great Emergency*, and *Ships That Pass in the Night*. Juna insisted that Ruth and her older sister Louisa read proper literary books, but she indulged their brother Jack's taste for *Tarzan* and *John Carter of Mars*. Juna's husband Mack read only the paper, but Ruth had seen him wink at Jack when their mother had been complaining about the books he read.

Juna had her good dress and shoes on one Saturday morning when she said, "I'm going to Mrs.

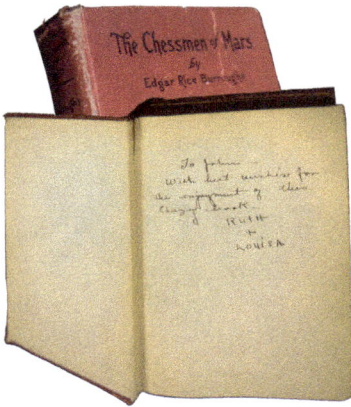

Hartnet's house. I'll be back at eleven." She leveled a stern look at Bonnie. "See that you and your sister read your lessons, young lady."

After Juna disappeared from sight up the elm-shaded street, Bonnie slammed her book shut, leaned back, and eyed the clouds scudding across the sky.

"Let's go upstairs and look at mother's books," Bonnie said. "I'll bet she doesn't have a single French book."

The girls checked the house to make sure Jack wasn't spying on them, then crept up the stairs to the ornate carved secretary in their parents' bedroom. It felt strange to be there by themselves.

"We shouldn't be here," Ruth whispered as she looked through the books, trying to picture her mother's thoughts as she read them.

"This is stupid," Bonnie said, showing Ruth *A Great Emergency*. "Let's go." On the endpapers, in the margins and between the lines of the book, Juna had written many schoolgirlish notes. She had treated the book as a secret diary that would never be discovered.

Ruth was fascinated. There was a note written on Valentine's Day, and in

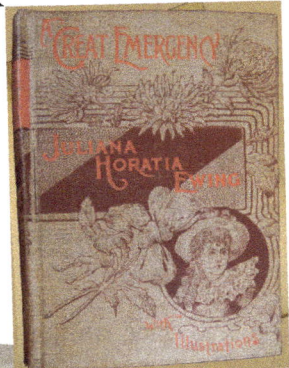

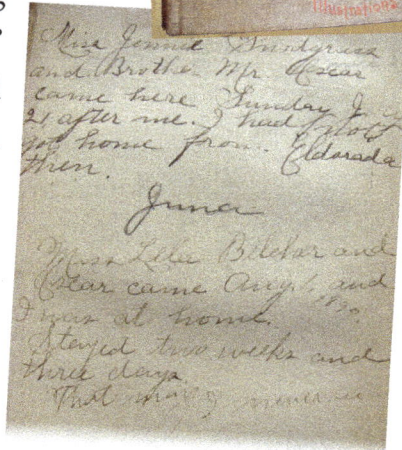

11

the back of the book was a picture of herself Juna had used as a bookmark. She'd written on the photo, "I am happier than I ever expected to be." It was dated June 10, 1898.

Ruth stared at the picture for a long time, trying to imagine her mother looking that way and thinking those thoughts. "I wonder if I will be happier than I expect to be," she thought.

"No French books," Bonnie said definitively. She marched Ruth back down to the rocking chairs on the porch and they worked on their French until their mother reappeared.

But as Ruth helped her mother make lunch she studied her face, looking for some sign of the person who had been 'happier than I ever expected to be,' but she saw only her mother's familiar face.

Jack romped in, waving a length of clothesline. "I'm *The Son of Tarzan*. Look!" He held up an Edgar Rice Burroughs book, the one he was currently enacting.

"Are you helping Tarzan with his laundry?" Bonnie grabbed at the clothesline, but Jack danced away.

"Evil tribesman tied me up. Simba saved me."

Juna glanced out the window. "Where are the shirts I had hanging on the line?"

Jack looked around innocently. "I stacked them."

"Go put the clothesline back up and bring the shirts in here right now."

Jack did as he was told. They heard Mack at the front door. "Lunch ready?" he called, sitting down at the table.

"It'll be on the table in just a moment," Juna said.

While Mack was reading the paper after lunch, he spotted an ad for a photographer. He read aloud the notice, *"One Day Only! Portraits taken this Saturday from one to five o'clock."* Juna responded with a smile and a nod. After Mack read the paper, he stretched out on the sofa and following his father's lead, Jack stretched out on the settee and they settled down for a short nap. Juna and Bonnie went to the store, and Ruth went up to her room and sat on the bed, gazing out the window as clouds glided across the clear blue sky. "I *will* be that happy," Ruth whispered to herself. The afternoon breeze stirred the oaks. Throughout her life, she would remember that particular afternoon when she realized she was responsible for her own life and her own happiness.

These days her mother seemed happiest in the garden. "When I grow up, I'll always have a garden," Ruth told herself, but it wasn't until the last years of her life that she did.

Saturday came and it was time for the kids to get cleaned up to have their picture taken by the photographer on Central Square. Juna was very particular that Jack had his tie straight and his hair neatly combed. Juna had Bonnie wear her sailor suit and she made Ruth put on her new hat and coat for the first picture, but she took them off for the last two photos. The photographer started oldest to youngest, and worked with his lively conversation and expression to get bright eyes and smiles. Bonnie felt she was too old and sophisticated to smile for the camera, but was still pleased with the results of her photos. Jack took his turn with a measure of success, and

Ruth thought the photographer was funny and had no trouble getting caught with a smile in all her photos.

When they got home, Ruth helped her mother boil tea and chip ice off the block in the icebox. Juna poured the brew into some tall glasses and they carried their iced tea to the porch and sat in the rocking chairs. "Read a little French for me," she said.

Ruth picked up the book she had been laboriously working through—*Dosia*—and began reading haltingly. After a while she stopped. "Did you and Dad ever go to France?"

Juna smiled. "Your father wanted to volunteer for the Great War but he was too old, thank the Lord. No, I've never been to Europe and never will." She smiled at her daughter. "Maybe you will."

The next morning Mack took Jack out to the little shed he used as a workshop. Four new and fragrant oak boards were laid out on the worktable.

"What are we going to build?" Jack asked.

"We're going to build you a bookshelf for all those books." He watched, fascinated, as his father neatly sawed off lengths of wood, and the two of them set to work making a bookcase.

"Scent of fresh-cut wood is nice isn't it?" his father said. "Two foot long should do it, don't you think?" Mack asked the boy. "Won't collect more books than that, will you?"

"I might," Jack said. "I plan to read all the Burroughs books."

When they had finished, they set the bookshelf up in his room and Jack neatly arranged his books on it.

Mack went downstairs to clean up the workshop. It would be wonderful collecting all the books Burroughs wrote, Jack thought, and having them lined up on the shelf. He lay on his bed admiring his books and drifted into sleep. Mack came up the stairs and stood for a moment looking at the neat row of books in the new bookcase and his son asleep on his bed, one leg hanging over the side. He smiled and tiptoed back down the stairs.

Throughout his life, Jack kept his Edgar Rice Burroughs books, lovingly glancing through them from time to time. In the late sixties, when Burroughs was again popular and paperback editions of his work with beautiful Frazetta and Krenkel covers

became available, his wife Doris would give them to Jack as birthday or anniversary gifts.

Mack told Juna he was going out on his real estate rounds, but instead drove to Sandstone cemetery. He found his father's grave near the hayfield fence and sat down on the ground, taking out the jar of moonshine he'd been hiding from Juna for so long. He took his hat off and raised a toast to his father.

The cicadas chirped and the breeze sighed in the trees along the fence line and through the hayfield where Mack had watched his father work all those years. He could see him now, in faded overalls and a wide straw hat, pitching hay up onto the wagon in slow steady arcs, the mules standing stock-still in the hot summer sun. "I know you loved the old farm, but me, I want something more." He took a taste of the liquor to remind him of his father.

Memories stirred of the first time his father had let him try moonshine. He'd bought it from Mathew Burnett at the feed store in Sandstone and let Mack touch his tongue to the rim of the pint jar. The first acrid fumes rising into his nose and the burn on his tongue had spurred his ten year old mind to wonder why anyone would want to drink moonshine.

Mack thought about the old house at the farm. He remembered watching the kids play outside, the times Bonnie rode the horse around the yard with great fanfare for her audience, little Jack and Ruth and sometimes the neighbor girl, all keeping a safe distance and feeling a bit fearful and envious.

17

He lifted up and shifted his weight on the solid ground. The dirt was hard here in Vernon County, prairie dirt. He set the jar down and stared into the distance for a long time. "You didn't discourage me from going into real estate, from selling the farm and moving into Nevada." He shrugged and rubbed the polished granite of the headstone, his finger tracing the words and dates cut into the stone. "Soon I want to move again. Up to Kansas City. That's where the money is." Across from the little cemetery, the field his father had worked all his life to keep neat and clean was already going back to prairie. But that's alright, Mack thought, it's the way of things. Nothing lasts forever. And he kind of liked seeing the old prairie returning, open and empty, like it had been when he was a boy.

Chapter 2

George was a bright, observant, and inquisitive child who liked to roam the fields by himself. He kept the things he did and saw to himself. Living on a small farm at the edge of the prairie, he was comfortable with silence. He was the only child of Grace and Lloyd Trial, born in December, 1910. His father would take him along to some of the Democratic Party meetings in nearby towns, and young George absorbed Lloyd's ability to project an easy conviviality at times, and to be entirely silent at others. George soon became the center of attention around adults, but he also liked his time alone, in the fields and in the parlor of the house where he grew up.

George also noticed the many compliments his father got for being the best dressed man in the room, with his pressed white Arrow shirts and brown and white wingtip shoes. Later in life, George was often the best dressed man in the room.

George (his mother called him Talbert) walked home from Muscotah Elementary school every day.

"What's the matter, Talbert?"

"Jimmy called me four-eyes."

"He don't mean nothing by it." She gave George a hug. He got into his chair at the table and she made cocoa for them both.

Do You Remember When?

George Talbert Trial

TWENTY TWO STUDENTS of the seventh and eighth grade classes at Muscotah posed outside the school for this shot in October of 1923.

"I told the teacher but she didn't do anything."

"Well, she's there to teach you; you have to get along among yourselves. That's something you need to learn."

"I don't want to wear glasses," he told his mother.

But she just shook her head. "It's better that you do. You can't see well enough without them."

George had always been a solitary person, and he was happy alone. His early days on the farm were idyllic, spent fishing in the creek with his father and helping his mother with the garden and with the milk cows and the chickens. From the farm at the edge of the prairie, world events seemed distant.

For the subsistence farmers in Muscotah County, the war in Europe in 1918 was a non-issue. No boys from Atchison County volunteered—they needed to work the farms. The local Sac and

Pottawatomie tribes had only been on their reservations twenty years. They held their annual pow-wows not far from Lloyd and Grace's farm, and Lloyd took George to see the tribesmen dance and sing in the light of great bonfires. The oldest men of the tribes could still remember a time when there were no Europeans in Kansas.

Grace Trial was a tiny woman, only five feet tall, soft-spoken. She was the daughter of George and Sarah Talbert, farmers who had moved to Kansas from Virginia soon after the Civil War and had done well. They owned over one hundred acres and kept their farm neat and well-worked.

The Talberts were all well-liked and respected by their neighbors, always willing to lend a hand with harvest, planting, calving, care of the draft animals, or repair of implements and buildings. Grace's father, George Talbert, was active in the Democratic Party, serving as an Atchison county commissioner from 1908 to 1912.

Grace was a quiet child, the youngest of three children. Her older brothers, James and Charles, had already moved out of the house, married, and started families of their own by the time she started high school. She graduated from the high school in Muscotah and then, like most farm girls of that era, worked at home, expecting to get married soon and move to her husband's farm. Her parents were protective of her. They sheltered their pretty, shy daughter from the boys who came around on one pretext or another, but they did not shelter her from hard work.

From earliest childhood she had chores she was expected to do. And she was a conscientious child; she did them without being told. She grew up working—in the garden, in the kitchen, and in the fields, helping with harvests and livestock. She worked hard and quietly, never complaining. Her parents tried to show her the better things in life, the things smart young women should know, including the game of golf.

The only fault the neighbors found in George and Sarah Talbert was that their church attendance was less regular than it should have been for someone of their standing in the community. Her parents took Grace to church often, but not regularly.

She soon learned that spirituality comes from one's own heart, not from a weekly sermon. Her parents taught her in their nonverbal way—by example—that hard work and consideration for one's family and friends are the best salvation, and that sometimes each person must suffer through hardship. She grew to be a caring, hard-working young woman who accepted her lot in life without complaint. She had only a distant knowledge of Christianity, but a great respect for learning.

Lloyd Trial was captivated by Grace's quiet beauty and large gray eyes. His parents' farm adjoined the Talbert farm, and frequently Lloyd spent the midday break from the fields at dinner with the Talberts. The meal was often served outside so the men would not bring their dirty clothes inside the house. And it was cooler under the big oak tree behind the house.

Grace helped her mother with the serving. Lloyd was handsome and outgoing, so it was easy for him to overcome Grace's shyness and strike up a conversation with her while he was helped fill buckets of water at the hand-pumped well. Although she was shy, she was clear in her views and opinions and very open-minded.

23

"I'm going to make something of myself," Lloyd told her frequently.

"You just make sure you get the hay cut this afternoon," was her standard reply.

Lloyd Trial

Lloyd grinned; he already had plans to go fishing in Delaware Creek with his buddies in the heat of the afternoon, while Mr. Talbert and the hired hands napped. They'd be back in time to help with the haying come evening. "It'll get done. No rain coming, so we've got plenty of time."

She smiled. "I see." And Lloyd knew she saw right through him.

Lloyd and Grace were married in the little Methodist church in Muscotah on an icy February Saturday in 1907. She was nineteen; he was twenty-three.

They farmed both the Trial farm and part of the Talbert farm for three years, then Lloyd's parents deeded their forty acres over to him, and George Talbert sold them the adjacent forty acres from his property. Grace and Lloyd now had eighty acres of their own—a big place by the standards of

Atchison County in 1910. In December of that same year, their son George was born.

Through the years that followed, Grace remained quiet and hard-working, practical and calm through even the worst calamities that regularly befall farmers—difficulties with crops and livestock. Lloyd tended to

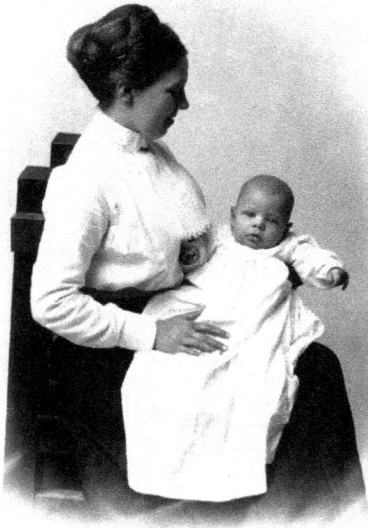

takes chances, but Grace was more conservative with money and was careful to keep them out of debt.

Lloyd worked hard at farming; but he had greater ambitions than just to be a successful farmer. He found pleasure in talking with the men in the feed stores and the dry goods stores in the little towns in western Atchison County where he'd go for farm supplies—tiny towns like Horton, Lancaster, Holton, Arrington, Huron, and Effingham. Driving the cart back to the farm, he thought about somehow getting into politics, getting elected to some office. He could do it. Everyone liked him, he was a good speaker, and he spoke knowledgeably about farming. He and Grace were happy and well-respected.

The stock market crash of 1929 had little effect on the subsistence farms of northeast Kansas. Lloyd, Grace, and their son George, like all the farmers in the area, lived almost entirely off their own land. They sold some milk, some hay, and an occasional side of beef. They bartered vegetables from each other's gardens in summer, helped each other with the crops, and loaned tools and equipment to each other. They grew vegetables in the summer and canned them for the winter. They raised chickens for eggs and meat, along with a few hogs and cows. Mule-drawn plows, threshing machines, and mowers were the norm. Lloyd had no motorized equipment, not even a car. In the whole county there was only one gas-powered John Deere tractor. George's parents still used a horse-drawn buggy to go into town for church and shopping and to go to the train depot when they visited Uncle Walter in Atchison.

Lloyd had learned the plasterer's trade from his father and had worked with him for several years, then he worked on the Missouri Pacific railroad bridge over the Missouri River at Atchison. When the bridge construction was done, he went to work for the Missouri Pacific as a brakeman on the Atchison to Forth Worth run. But he hated being away from home so much. He came back to the farm, joined the Democratic Party, and was chosen as a delegate to the convention in Wichita his first year as a party member. He worked hard, but still took time to go fishing with his friends. While they sat on the bank of the creek, the talk would often turn to politics and Lloyd found he enjoyed that. His friends listened to his opinions and he decided to try for the local postmaster position, the first step in what could be a political career that might reach as far as the capitol in Wichita. In those days even the tiniest town had a post office and the postmaster position was a political patronage position—a potential stepping-stone to elected offices. He'd confide his ambitions to his son George as they sat on the bank of Perry Lake.

"George, I want you to go to college," Lloyd said. "I can save enough money to get you into St. Benedict's college in Atchison. You can live with your uncle during the semester, and come back here to help your mother and me with the farm on your vacations."

George was very close to his outgoing, popular father, and he hated the idea of being away from home. But he had been taught not to complain. His mother would not tolerate complaints. Riding with his father down the dusty country roads from one town to the next on Party business, Lloyd would sometimes ask George to holds the reins while he massaged his forehead. Sometimes, when they went fishing together on the shady bank of Perry Lake, Lloyd had to stop and lie down because his head hurt.

It was supper time and George was nowhere to be seen. Grace stepped out onto the wide veranda and scanned the pasture for him. Lloyd put down the Atchison Enquirer and joined her. He put his arms around her waist. "He'll be coming along soon, we don't need to worry. He's a reliable boy."

Grace pushed his hands away. "What if the neighbors see us?"

He smiled that handsome smile that had won her heart. "Let them be jealous."

Grace spotted her son making his way up the pasture from the tree line at the little wet-weather creek. After Lloyd had gone back to his paper she watched George coming steadily across the fields toward the house. She worried about his silences. He was a sociable boy, playing easily with the other kids at school, but after school he would spend his time by himself or in the parlor looking through books and old Collier's magazines. He never said anything about how he felt, what he wanted, what he thought.

She shook her head and went inside to put the dinner on the table. Just like his father—sociable and outgoing around others, but when he's alone or with me, he's a very private man. She ladled gravy into the gravy bowl.

George dutifully washed his hands at the pump, then came inside to the supper table. He was a polite boy, his parents insisted on that, but he also had the assumptions of an only child—that everything would be as he wanted it to be.

In summers George roamed the farm; through the hot hay field, fescue, and lespedeza, into the trees at the fence line where the Guernsey cows stood in the shade batting flies and chewing. He was observant of nature—the color of a dragonfly's wing, the pale purple flower of a thistle. He enjoyed their small farm and felt a certain peace in staring at the sunset, and the pleasant melancholy

that would come over him. He would eventually characterize that melancholy as the silent, loving touch of the land itself. George did not know it then, not until later in his life, when some pain and loss had touched him, but many years later he would recognize that silent feeling for what it was—contentedness. He came to know that feeling as the most lasting happiness anyone could have. Elation would evaporate quickly, thrills more quickly still, but contentment could be found silently emanating from an interesting, challenging activity. And the world was full of such activities.

He amused himself in the hayloft, sometimes sitting on the edge swinging his feet and watching the warped dance of heat of midday August. He was content to spend time alone even though Grace had taken him to Jimmie Butler's house a few times. The boys played together and seemed to enjoy themselves, but George never asked to go there.

After school Lloyd would take George to the general store and let him amuse himself there while Lloyd attended to business at the post office next door. George entertained the men sitting in the cool and fragrant store, farmers who had come in to get this part or that and were eager for a break and some socializing. George talked easily; he liked to be the center of attention. "Ain't he just like Lloyd though?" the men would remark. "Always got just the right words."

The days drifted by.

In high school George socialized easily and superficially with his gawky classmates from the farms surrounding the thriving community of Muscotah. He liked reading and his grades were good, especially in history and geography. He also liked biology, but that subject he had to study. The rest came easy, most of it he already knew from having read atlases and history books that Grace brought home from the Muscotah library. But George also liked the long walk home by himself, his mind drifting off

into reverie along the familiar route. At the farm he would change into his work clothes and go about his chores, helping his mother with the cattle.

George stood on the front steps of the Muscotah High School. His father would sometimes meet him there in his stylish hat and Arrow shirt, his brown and white shoes neatly polished. He had a car, but now he preferred to drive the

buggy to the post office every day. George liked the way people looked at his father as they drove down Muscotah's quiet streets, the men often tipping their hats. Everyone knew Lloyd Trial—George came to expect that, and to like it. Everyone knew his father and everyone knew his father would achieve great things.

But that day Lloyd was not there. George waited for a while, then started walking down the familiar streets, his mind elsewhere, daydreaming. He loved to walk—the even pace of his feet, his breathing, the swing of his arms, the world slowly moving past. The simple act of walking took him to a magic world, his own world that somehow was at one with the world around him, with the scent of lilac and the warmth of the sun between tree shade.

At the cemetery the flags were up for Decoration Day. George noticed there was a horse and buggy standing in the shade of an old elm. It was his father's buggy, empty. The horse stood there

motionless, then shook his head and whickered in greeting as he smelled George approaching. George stroked the animal's neck. That was when he caught sight of his father sitting, hat off, head down, near one of the gravestones. George started forward, then paused and stood for a full minute. His father didn't move, he just sat there looking down at the grass. Then he set his hat down and massaged his temples for a moment. A moment more and he got to his feet and started back toward the buggy. George melted into the hedge and waited until his father had gone. That evening he examined his father's face at the dinner table, but saw only the familiar handsome smile.

In May 1927, George Talbert Trial graduated from Muscotah High School. After the ceremony, everyone filed out of the hot brick building into a silky June evening. George kept his gown and mortarboard on and held his diploma in a sweat-dampened hand as they made their way through the chattering crowd. His mother was beaming, but she didn't hug him—that was not her way. Lloyd was the center of a small group of men talking politics, as always. He broke free and came over to George, put his arm around his shoulders, and shook his hand briskly. "I'm proud of you."

Later they climbed into the buggy and rode out of town to the big house at the curve of the gentle hill. Grace brought lemonade out on a silver tray her mother had given her and used the cut glass pitcher and glasses she normally used only for Reverend Beasley's monthly visits. They sat in the glider on the veranda.

The next morning George was up at dawn as usual. His mother was gathering eggs. "I'd like you to milk the cows, Talbert," she told him. He went to the barn, closed the stanchion on the Guernseys, and milked them. He poured off the milk into the milk can and lugged it up to the well house to keep it cool until the milk truck came around later in the morning to pick it up. He climbed up the rough ladder to the loft and pitched a forkful of hay down to the cattle. Then he carefully put the pitchfork back on the nails driven into the wall and sat down on the edge of the loft door, looking at the clear morning and the grass drenched in dew, daydreaming.

The ringing of the iron triangle roused him to come in for

breakfast. At the table his father was already eating, a napkin tucked into his white Arrow shirt. It was clear his mother and father had been arguing, and he knew it had been about him. George ate quickly and excused himself to go haul buckets of water from the cistern to the watering trough.

After his father's buggy had made its way down the gravel lane toward town, George went over to where his mother was weeding the beans in the garden. "I don't mind working the farm by myself," he told her. "In fact I want to. I'll make a success of it, you'll see."

She straightened slowly, holding her back. She adjusted her bonnet. "I know you will, Talbert. And maybe you should for a while, give your father time to…do the things he wants to do." She looked at her tiny house, then stared at the flat plane of prairie already hazy with heat. "But there's a whole wide world, Talbert, and the way to see it is by getting an education, getting a good job, making something of yourself."

"Farming is good. Granddad did alright," he threw back at her.

She smiled at his obvious tactic. "My father worked hard all his life to build this acreage. He's proud of it, and he should be, but these days he's told me more than once he wished he'd seen more of the world while he was young. He's old now and that chance is gone. I don't want your chance to be gone before you know it."

George toed some dirt around. "I like school…but the money…"

"You let your father and me worry about the money. Uncle Walter has already said you could board at his house in Atchison, help him some; he's gone riding the trains to Texas a lot. He'd be happy to have you, and his house is walking distance to the college."

In spite of himself, George saw himself on campus, reading geography and history, his favorite topics. He wiped the grin off his face. "Well, I'll work the farm this year. Dad said he needs the time to do his Democratic Party work. Maybe a year from this September I could go to St. Benedict, or…"

"A year from this autumn," his mother said softly but firmly. George went down to the barn to get the cantankerous mule-drawn

36

sickle ready to cut hay. He knew his mother well enough to know that when she said something in that tone, it would happen.

Memorial Day 1930, six in the morning, and George was preparing the mule team to cut hay. There were clouds in the west, and he didn't want it to rain on the hay. Lloyd was up early too; he was the chairman of the Memorial Day celebration. George heard him practicing his speech.

"...a new brick high school. A new post office, a gas pump in front of Wehmeyer's store. We have progress the way it should be—steady and dependable. Let the Wall Street tycoon suffer." George recognized it as the same speech Lloyd had used at the Grange Hall in April. "Here in Muscotah we'll make our own fortune by hard work, the way we always have. We don't borrow money, we don't invest in European stocks, we don't buy oil shares. We grow hay and cattle and we'll continue to do so while Mr. Hoover gets the nation back on track."

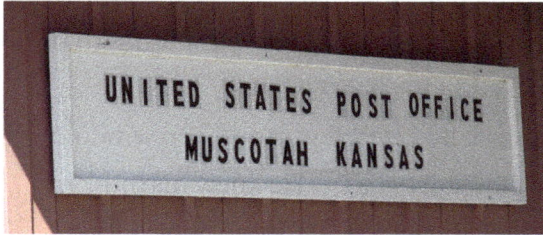

By the time he had the hay cut and raked, the clouds had disappeared, so George cleaned himself up and walked the four blocks to the center of town. He sat with his mother in the folding chairs in the shady part of the town square while his father and the other dignitaries gave their speeches. George wore his brown suit from Harzfeld's in Kansas City, along with a pressed white shirt, and as the crowd milled and talked after the speeches, he liked the looks he got from the girls.

George ran the farm now. Lloyd spent all his time on the road for the Democratic Party. He hoped to be appointed the Muscotah postmaster. George noticed the look Lloyd would give the new post office every time they rode by together.

George had a wide-ranging curiosity and intelligence, which he satisfied with books from the Muscotah library. But he was also a dreamer. He had a wide range of interests—history, geography, medicine, science. He had an easy way with words, was articulate and outgoing, but always retained an internal silence, something he learned from the land and his father as a boy, something that would keep certain things locked in his heart.

He also liked to go to Kansas City every few months to window shop and sometimes to buy a new shirt or a tie. He knew his mother and father still talked about his education. "It's important, Lloyd," he'd heard his mother say one evening. "You say it yourself in your speeches."

Lloyd lowered his newspaper slightly. "And that's the point, Talbert graduated from that high school, his grades were good, the teachers all said so. Now he's working this farm and doing it well. He can wait a few more months. After I'm postmaster we can get the Henderson boys to work the farm for us. They've asked about it before. They're looking for land to work shares."

"And working shares will still give us all we need to live and your salary can go for…"

Lloyd raised his hand to cut off the words. "I know—meetings and trips, which are necessary for the party and for my career."

Grace knew enough to stop speaking.

By September George was a freshman at St. Benedict's College in Atchison. Lloyd realized his dream in 1932 when he competed against four other candidates for the Muscotah postmaster, and won the position.

TRIAL RECEIVES MUSCOTAH P. O.

Well Known Democrat Is Awarded Position By Postmaster General

Lloyd Trial is the new postmaster of Muscotah.

His appointment arrived yesterday, by letter, from James H. Farley, postmaster general.

Mr. Trial will succedd R. E. Ellson, Republican, resigned, who has held office since July, 1930.

Mr. Trial was one of a field of five candidates for the Muscotah postoffice. The other four were: M. L. Roach, a former postmaster of Muscotah; W. H. Comer, Mrs. C. M. Lukens and Alvin Henning.

Lloyd Trial was born at Muscotah, April 27, 1884. He has lived there his entire life. He was educated in the Rose Hill and Muscotah schools. He learned the plasterer's trade under his father, W. H. Trial, when a boy. Later he took up bridge and building construction work in Atchison county, and remained in that work for eight years. Still later, for eight years, he was a Missouri Pacific brakeman out of Atchison. During the Woodring administration he was with the Kansas state grain department.

Mr. Trial belongs to a Democratic family. His first political recognition came in 1920, when he was chosen a delegate to the Democratic state convention in Wichita. He has always been a Democrat and actively engaged in party work. Last year he was elected precinct committeeman, and campaigned for the general ticket last fall.

Mr. Trial has the distinction of being the third Democratic postmaster in the history of Muscotah. Four generations of the Trial family have been active Democrats.

Chapter 3

The cramped dining room in the house in Kansas City was nothing like the big rooms and high ceilings of the house at 305 Central Avenue in Nevada, Ruth mused over dinner. She was

305 Central Avenue; Nevada, Missouri

eager to eat and go to her room, since her mother and father had been bickering throughout the meal. "Times are going to get bad," Juna said for the tenth time. Mack pushed his plate back and signaled Ruth for some coffee.

"We'll be fine," Mack said. "Bonnie's teaching, Jack's a runner with the Kansas City Southern Railway."

"You saw the newspaper," Juna continued. "Bank holiday again. Unemployment is already twice what it was last summer."

"We'll get along fine," Mack reassured her. "People got to eat. Cattlemen will bring stock to the stockyards and railroads will haul them to the packing houses in Chicago. All those employees will have to live somewhere in Kansas City." He got up and got the paper from the parlor, giving Ruth a reassuring smile as he passed. He held a page of the paper up to Juna. "J. C. Nichols is building houses right now."

Juna squinted at the paper as though it was a mouse in a mousetrap. "I'll be saying extra prayers that Bonnie and Jack keep their jobs. And I won't hear of taking our savings and buying a house to resell."

"Anyway, we sold the big house in Nevada just at the right time," Mack said. He was proud of the deal he'd made for the house at 4410 Garfield Avenue. They owned the Kansas City house free and clear and still had two thousand dollars in the bank.

4410 Garfield Avenue; Kansas City, Missouri

Ruth cleared off the empty plates. "I'm going to my room now, to study."

Mack smiled at her. "I'm glad you've gotten started at Kansas City Junior College."

41

Ruth nodded, feigning enthusiasm. In her room Ruth lay on the bed but didn't open her schoolbooks. Instead she remembered how she had felt back in Nevada when first her sister, and then her brother had left for Kansas City. She'd cried and cried, feeling like she was being abandoned. Now they were all together again, but it didn't feel the same. "I guess I'm not the girl I used to be," she thought. Outside, the crickets chirped in the soft summer evening. She dozed and dreamed she was back at the farm in Sandstone, before they'd moved to town.

She remembered the smell of the grass on summer afternoons, the warmth of the sun when she'd helped her mother in the garden. She'd only been eight when they'd moved to town, but she remembered every tree and flower of that old farm.

Her mother had kept a garden behind the house on Central Avenue in Nevada,

but here in Kansas City there was no room for a garden. Ruth sat up and opened her biology textbook. Now her mother spent her time at the nearby Oak Grove Methodist Church. Mack still occasionally looked for real estate deals, but he was too old for a market already crowded with young men looking for deals. There were houses for sale, but the banks were only open Tuesdays and Thursdays and no home mortgage loans were being made for ninety days, the newspaper told them. After dinner most evenings, Mack would read The Kansas City Star, but he no longer commented on the articles or the economic recovery that 'was already starting to take shape.' Juna read her bible. For a few months, Ruth had had to stay in the kitchen washing and drying the dishes while her parents would go through their daily quarrel over Mack's desire to use their savings to buy a house to resell. Juna was adamant they hold onto their money. Now, Mack was silent.

Ruth liked taking the bus to Kansas City Junior College. The classes weren't too difficult. She liked to read but had no interest in studying. She had enrolled in a series of courses in physical education since they involved the least homework.

Jack was his normal sunny self. "Working for the railroad's the best job ever," he'd tell them every Thursday evening when he came by for dinner.

"Take your hat off, Jack," his mother told him. "You look like a reporter wearing your hat like that at the dinner table."

Jack sailed his hat onto the sofa while his mother rolled her eyes. "One day I'll be riding the rails myself, see the world," Jack said, cheerfully oblivious to any bad feelings around him.

Sometimes in the evening, just to get out of the house, Ruth would take a walk through the pleasant streets of the neighborhood. The neighborhood was friendly and reasonably prosperous even in these hard times. She liked the long sweep of Troost Avenue, with its streetcar tracks and neighborhood shops, but she liked the narrow grassy park that separated the north and south lanes of Paseo Boulevard best.

Some Saturday mornings Ruth and Bonnie would take the streetcar all the way downtown to window shop Emery, Bird, Thayer department store or have coffee and cake at the second floor coffee shop in the Jones store over looking 12th Street. People may have been losing their jobs in New York, but here in Kansas City things weren't so bad.

Sometimes they'd go the other direction to the Spanish-themed shopping area J. C. Nichols had built along Brush Creek named the Country Club Plaza. Between their house and the Plaza, the Nelson Art Gallery had recently been completed—a gift to the city from Kansas City's leading citizen, William Rockhill Nelson, the publisher of The Kansas City Star. Juna was thrilled that they could walk to a great gallery and see world-class works of art.

As the depression deepened, the Wallace family tightened their belts. But luckily they had no mortgage payments to make, and Bonnie's teaching job at Westwood View School brought in a good salary. Jack, now twenty years old, was also able to contribute money to the family from his work at the Kansas City Southern Railway. Things were not so bad.

Ruth woke at the sound of the front door closing. She heard the click of high heels; Bonnie was home from her date. Ruth smiled as she heard her sister pause, take her shoes off, then pad to the basement stairs and go down. Ruth pulled on a robe and went down to the basement after her. Only the dim light in the corner by the coal scuttle was on. She smelled cigarette smoke. "Close the door," Bonnie said. Ruth dutifully pulled the door closed. Bonnie was in her easy chair beside the coal furnace, cigarette in hand. She looked older than her thirty years and Ruth thought of the ambitious and determined Bonnie back in Nevada

"Lot of stupid men around here," Bonnie said. "Give up my career and get married—that's what people expect. But I can't quit, we need the money. Dad will never work again. He's too old for real estate and that's all he knows." She dragged deep on her Chesterfield and blew smoke at the dusty ductwork.

"I can work," Ruth said. "I don't need to go to Junior College."

"Yes you do," Bonnie snapped, and Ruth subsided.

"These stupid men seem to think I should be grateful just because they take me down to the Pla-Mor to drink and dance, or eat a cheap steak dinner at the Majestic." She stubbed her cigarette out. "But they have nothing to talk about because they know nothing."

"You'll find the right guy…"

"Don't become a teacher," Bonnie continued. She pulled another cigarette out of the pack.

"You have a great job at Westwood View," Ruth said. At that moment Ruth realized that in all the years since they'd moved to Kansas City, she'd never seen the same man come back for a second date with Bonnie. She knew her older sister's intensity, her intelligence—was that such a liability to happiness?

"You know something?" Bonnie continued in the same level tone. Ruth braced herself for more bad news. "I should never have gone into teaching. I don't really like kids, never did. Being around them all day, every day has reinforced that. I'll get married, but I'll never have kids."

"You may change…" Ruth said.

"We all change. But I won't change my mind about that." came her rapid fire reply.

It was going to make it even more difficult for Bonnie to get married if she insisted on not having kids. For some reason the image of Bonnie facing down the cow in the pasture when they had been kids on the farm at Sandstone came to Ruth's mind. Bonnie's fearlessness now seemed more like bitterness.

Ruth started making it a habit to take their dog Judy out for a long walk while Bonnie was eating breakfast, but Ruth always liked to be home when her brother Jack came by for dinner, usually Thursday evening, the day before his weekly payday. He'd breezily recount the railroad stories he heard that week. A hundred trains a week came through Kansas City, where four rail lines converged to exchange freight. Jack's job as a runner was to carry messages throughout the giant railroad complex. He liked the job; it gave him a chance to visit all of the offices, yards, and shops in the river bottoms near the stockyards. Every week he'd come home with new railroad stories (many of which, Ruth thought,

47

sounded more like tall tales). But it was easy to see why people at the railroad liked Jack. He was smart, cheerful, gregarious, and hard-working. He was soon given freight clerk duties in addition to his runner duties, and he excelled at them, too. He was a sharp dresser, and his hair was already thinning, making him look older than his twenty-six years.

Many nights Ruth tossed and turned, troubled by the changes she saw in her big sister. She stared out the window at the stars in the night sky. I guess I've changed too, she thought. But I'm still a dreamer. When her sister had called her that in the past it had irritated her a little. Now it seemed comforting.

Sixty miles north of Kansas City, at St. Benedict's College in Atchison, Kansas, George Trial was a sophomore, studying biology with hopes of becoming a doctor. He lived in an upstairs room of his Uncle Walter's house on Maple Street in Atchison, only three blocks from where Amelia Earhart's grandparents' house stood. Atchison was a thriving town. Farmers sold their grain at the row of concrete grain elevators that stood alongside the Atchison, Topeka, and Santa Fe tracks. George's uncle, Walter Talbert, was a scheduler for the railroad and worked long hours in late summer when the harvest was coming in.

St. Benedict's had been built sixty years earlier as a Benedictine monastery. In the late 1920s they had added classrooms and became a college.

At a nearby sweeping overlook, George's favorite place at school, he often sat on a bench and watched the river roll by while daydreaming of far away places, his imagination fired by the geography and history courses he was taking. The breeze was cool and steady, scented with the hot fields beyond. The unknown pulled at him with its infinite promise. He imagined Europe, Asia, and the ancient empires of the Middle East—the Sumerians, the Chaldeans, the Hittites—familiar names from the bible that he had heard and read about all his life. But now he saw them as real people, living and dying in real cities, not cardboard figures from a Sunday school lesson. The visions of other lands and other people played incessantly in his head. He knew he needed to get back to his stuffy second floor room in his uncle's house, get back to his chemistry homework, but the breeze out over the land was too intoxicating.

He had read the entire history textbook in the first two weeks of class and the tests were a snap. But biology and chemistry were hard. He had to work to keep up with the boys who'd gone to high school in Atchison, St. Joe, and Kansas City. The one-room elementary school he'd attended had taught him reading, writing, and arithmetic, but little else. Mrs. Ballew, the sixth grade teacher at the Muscotah school, was a stickler for penmanship though, and George had learned it well. The monks who taught at St. Benedict's also required that students have excellent penmanship, and throughout his life George's handwriting was clear, strong, and graceful.

After daydreaming on the bench, George strolled down the shady streets to his room to continue his studies. The first semester had been hard—not knowing anyone and being older than the other boys. But George was smart and articulate; he forced himself to get out and meet the other boys. He didn't care anything for sports, but played baseball just to be on the team. By the end of his freshman year, he was enjoying himself so much that he hated for school to be over. But he went back to the farm at Muscotah and worked hard all summer. In the evenings he was exhausted from work, but he still had energy enough to read the books he checked out of the tiny Muscotah library.

When summer was over, he was happy to be back in his upstairs room at Uncle Walter's house and back in class. The fall semester of 1933 sped by. But just a few days before Christmas, George's world ended.

At the house of his in-laws in Muscotah, George's father Lloyd sat in the comfortable blue serge armchair staring at the snow-covered fields outside. He thought of all the tiny outlying towns he'd visited so many times while working for the Democratic Party. He'd been active in the party for years. He'd been the youngest delegate at the state convention in Wichita in 1921. His hard work had paid off; in addition to farming, he had been appointed Postmaster of the Muscotah Post Office, a political patronage job and a good stepping stone to a future in politics. His father-in-law had been county commissioner for Atchison County twenty years ago, and Lloyd had aspirations greater than that. He studied his father-in-law's guns on their racks over the fireplace—a beautiful Colt forty-five revolver and two matched Winchester 30-06 lever action rifles. Lloyd's head hurt, as it often did these days, which is why he had stayed home while his wife Grace and his parents-in-law had gone to a Christmas party at their neighbor's farm just three miles down the road. Lloyd sat waiting for his headache to ease, with strange, uneasy thoughts running through his head. He pushed them aside and tried to concentrate on fishing in the hot summer days down by Delaware Creek or Perry Lake. He could visualize the shape of the bank, where he would stand, where he would cast. The water was still and cool and inviting. He and his son George used to go fishing almost every week when George had been a boy. That was ten years ago.

The pain in his head was getting steadily worse. He had not discussed it with Grace—or with anyone else—he didn't want to compromise his chances for his future political career. He squeezed his eyes shut for a few moments. When he opened them, his vision jumped with each slow beat of his heart. "I'm only forty-seven," he thought, "but I feel twice that age." He got up carefully and leaned against the mantle. After a few minutes he took down the Colt pistol. It was loaded, he noticed. He sat back down in the chair and stared at the gun, then at the frozen empty fields. After a while he lifted it to his head and squeezed the trigger.

The next day, December 22, 1933, the sky in northeastern Kansas was overcast, and a sharp wind was blowing from the west. George knew it would snow again soon. He was planning to return to Muscotah to spend Christmas with his parents tomorrow, but he'd use today to study. He had not done well on his chemistry and physiology courses—a C and a D. He heard the phone ring downstairs and his uncle talking to someone. Phones were rare. His uncle had one so he could contact the railroad dispatch office if

he needed to. But phone calls this late at night were not common. George kept at his studies. After a while he heard his uncle slowly climbing the worn wooden stairs. He knocked and came in, an expression on his face that George had never seen before. Walter fumbled his pipe out of his pocket and turned it over and over in his hands. "Come downstairs for a minute Talbert," he said.

George followed him down to the too warm kitchen where Walter always sat after dinner smoking his pipe. They never used the sitting room with its doilies and overstuffed chairs. His uncle had once told him that his aunt thought they were too good to sit on. George forced himself to sit down across the table from his uncle, suddenly very tense.

"We've had some bad news."

"Something wrong at the farm? An accident?" George said, tension rising.

"Your father is dead I'm afraid."

"What happened?" George asked, surprised by his own calmness.

His uncle stared at the table. "We don't know yet; gunshot wound."

George heard the old clock ticking out in the dusty parlor. There was no other sound.

"I've made some fresh coffee," Walter said, but George didn't hear. He stood and looked around the room, trying to get his bearings. "There's nothing you can do tonight." There was no phone at the farm, so George could not call his mother.

"Mother's alright?" Uncle Walter nodded. They sat at the table for a while. Walter offered to play cards with him to occupy his mind, but George said he wanted to go upstairs and lie down.

Walter pulled out his pocket watch. "Try to get some sleep. I'll go with you to the farm tomorrow." George nodded, then went upstairs and packed his worn carpetbag, the one his father had given him when he'd first come to Atchison two years ago. He lay down and to his own surprise slept through the night.

The next morning he and his uncle walked through the fresh-fallen snow to the stable where Walter kept his carriage and horse. They stepped into the train station so Walter could buy a

ILL HEALTH AS SUICIDE CAUSE

That's Given as Explanation of Act of Lloyd Trial, Muscotah

Worry over ill health is believed to have caused the suicide late yesterday afternoon of Lloyd Trial, 49 postmaster of Muscotah, at the home of his father-in-law, the late George Talbert, adjoining the Trial property at the north edge of that city.

Mr. Trial was alone when he took his own life with a revolver and had been dead only a short time when his body was found. He had been known to have worried recently over the state of his health but none of his friends had the slightest inkling that he would take his life.

A member of the pioneer family of William H. Trial of Muscotah, who have lived in Muscotah since they came to Kansas in 1878, Lloyd Trial enjoyed a wide circle of friends in Northeastern Kansas. He was a staunch Democrat and so is his father.

Lloyd Trial was born at Muscotah April 27, 1884. He was educated in the Muscotah public schools and early in life learned the plasterer's trade, which he followed a number of years. Later he was employed in bridge and building work by Atchison county and during the administration of former Governor Harry Woodring served in the Kansas State Grain Inspection office in Atchison.

February 16, 1907, Mr. Trial married Miss Grace Talbert of Muscotah, who survives with one son, Talbert Trial, 23 years old. Other survivors are his parents and seven brothers and sisters as follows: Melvin D. Trial, Tulsa, Okla., Richard H. Trial, Atchison; Mrs. Elizabeth Stewart, Klamath Falls, Ore.; Mrs. Lillian Alban, Huron; Mrs. Nellie Hale, Winston, Mont., Mrs. Grace Roach, Muscotah, and Mrs. Lola Young, Omaha, Nebraska.

Funeral services will be conducted at the Congregational church in Muscotah tomorrow afternoon at 2:30 o'clock and the officiating minister will be the Rev. Jesse W. Foster. There will be a Masonic service at the grave in the Muscotah cemetery. Leslie Hubbard of the Harouff & Buis Funeral home is in charge of arrangements.

newspaper while the stable hands harnessed the horse and brought the carriage around. There was a short article in the Atchison Globe.

"Don't let this get into your mind too much, George. You need to concentrate on helping your mother and finishing your schooling."

George stared at the newspaper article until the carriage was brought around and they made the long, cold trip to the farm.

Walter and George found Grace's house full of relatives presided over by Reverend Beasley. The coroner talked with George for a moment, but the little man in black was in a hurry to get back to his family in Atchison for Christmas. The questions he asked seemed too personal to George. He had never discussed emotions with either of his parents, and certainly not depression.

George and Walter helped Grace with the chores. Grace's friends came by one after another for most of the afternoon. They brought pies and baked chickens, canned beans and cranberries, rhubarb and fresh-baked bread. The table was loaded.

The funeral was the day before Christmas. Everyone in the community attended. The preacher quoted the usual passages to reassure them of life eternal, but the unspoken question hovered in the rafters of the crowded church: why had Lloyd done it? A man with the intelligence and ambition of Lloyd—gone.

Reverend Beasley insisted Grace meet with him and his family every evening and Grace acquiesced, but George flatly refused. Grace found Beasley's ministrations more irritating than comforting, but for a week she dutifully spent an hour with him praying and reading from the bible. The rest of the day she kept busy. Farm life is governed by routines, and routines helped occupy her mind. She felt lonely at night lying in her bed alone. She would hear the 9:40 train in the distance and had to work hard to keep her mind from dwelling on all that had happened.

Mornings were better. She would rise before dawn, put coal in the stove, attend to chores, and then make coffee, bacon, and eggs. She kept the same routine that she had kept when Lloyd was alive, although she cancelled the Atchison Globe newspaper subscription. Seeing the newspaper rolled up on the table just the way it had been when Lloyd was alive was more than she could bear. Lloyd had taken a lot of pleasure in unrolling the fresh newspaper, drinking his coffee, and commenting on the articles while they ate breakfast together.

After lunch she would lie down for a nap the way she always had. Her dreams were the same as always—thinking about the farm work that needed to be done; not fretting, just planning. In the evenings she sewed. She didn't ask for help, although her neighbors continually offered. She did ask her friends Lois and Alice to dispose of Lloyd's clothes, though. She could not bring herself to look in the closet. The suits and Arrow shirts that he was so proud of, his work clothes, the straw hat he used to wear to go fishing.

George could easily see that his mother needed the routine of farm work. He let her continue with the milking and feeding, cooking and cleaning, even though she looked exhausted. The day after Christmas, Walter returned to Atchison. Grace continued to meet with Beasley each evening. While she was away, George would bring in three buckets of coal for the night and throw a piece in the stove from time to time until she returned. He would sit and stare at the black iron door with its eight small glass panes smoked almost black. He would sit watching the orange glow behind the smoky lenses—not thinking, not daydreaming, just sitting, trying to absorb the knowledge that the future had forever changed.

He tried to make himself comfortable with the idea of living in this house again, working on the farm like he had, living in the slow turning of the seasons. Other futures seemed elusive, already slipping away. He had wanted to become a doctor, maybe go to medical school in Kansas City, perhaps live there one day. But now...

He missed his father, but it was not something one talked about. Three days after New Year's he came in from the morning chores and found his mother had made waffles on the big cast iron waffle iron. This usually signaled a celebration of some sort.

"Uncle Walter told me classes start tomorrow," she said. George stared at his coffee cup, a heavy china mug painted with an improbable Alpine scene.

"Yes."

"Then we need to leave today after dinner. One o'clock at the latest. I need to get some flour and bacon in Atchison at the store. If we leave by one I can be back by milking time."

George and his mother rode the carriage through a clear winter afternoon to Atchison. He helped her get her supplies at the store, then he hoisted his carpetbag out of the carriage and stood watching her ride away.

From time to time for the rest of his life, George would remember that moment with gratitude—the moment his mother had allowed him to go back to school, letting him walk away from the farm, and from her, and out into the wide world.

Chapter 4

It never occurred to Grace to ask for help with the farm, nor did it occur to her neighbors not to help. That was the way farming was done in those days.

The cattle and chickens were fed, and when spring came, the hay and the corn and the soybeans were planted. In June the hay was cut and hauled and the garden was planted and weeded. The community had always worked their farms together; there was no other way farming could be done with mule-drawn implements and hand labor.

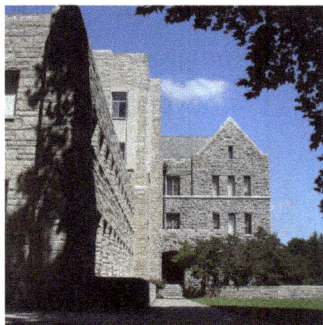

George graduated from St. Benedict's at the end of May, 1934 with an associate of arts degree. His mother and Uncle Walter made their way to the lawn in front of the imposing stone buildings and sat on folding chairs during the ceremony. Grace sat beside her brother listening respectfully to the speeches, a little intimidated by the people around her. After the ceremony George had trouble finding Grace, her five foot figure dwarfed by the crowd of big farm-bred people around her. But he spotted Uncle Walter and there she was standing beside him, beaming.

"I'm proud of you," she said. She and George didn't hug, a little embarrassed by all those around them who did. Uncle Walter shook his hand, then the three of them walked down the hill to Walter's house, where George put his diploma on the dining room table. They went out to lunch in the big restaurant in the train station. Afterward, George and Grace took the 2:45 train back to Muscotah and walked the last mile to the farm. George found his mother had baked a gooseberry pie for him.

The next morning George did his chores, came in to eat eggs and biscuits, then started cutting hay. He cut the hay with a mule-drawn sickle bar cutter, sheaved it by hand, and hauled it to the loft in the wagon.

He helped his mother milk the cows twice a day and wean the calves. He helped weed the corn, tomatoes, beans, strawberries, and squash in the garden. He fed the chickens and collected eggs.

Every morning George harnessed the old horse, Willie, and took the buggy into town with the eggs and milk for sale at the store. He closed his mind to everything except the endless round of farm work.

The Atchison County Democratic Party chairman came down to Muscotah soon after Lloyd's death. He offered his condolences to Grace, then took George aside and said the party was offering George the opportunity to finish out his father's term as postmaster of the Muscotah post office.

"It's an honor, George. And a token of how we all felt about your father."

Without really thinking much about it, George accepted the position. He worked hard to keep the post office and the farm running right. He had no time to think and that was the way he wanted it. Summer came, and with it, farm work intensified. It was the end of June before George had any time for himself. Until then, he had not attended church services even though his mother went every Sunday. He told her he had too much work to do, but in reality, he didn't want to see the half-sympathetic, half-horrified looks of his neighbors. What would the son of a suicide turn out to be?

Then one Sunday in June, George rode in the carriage with his mother to the Muscotah church. It was sweltering hot, everyone fanning themselves with paper fans printed with Omaha Feed and Supply advertisements. George mouthed the words during the hymns, and the sermon went in one ear and out the other, but he did notice there were quite a few young women there, all looking very nice in their white summer dresses. Afterward, the Reverend Beasley had set up a lemonade table under the oak trees. George bought one glass, then another. He chatted with the girls serving the lemonade until his mother finally came looking for him.

"Land's sake, Talbert! We can't stay here all day."

The next Sunday George was back. He learned the name of an attractive brunette—Virginia Chavet. They started seeing each other in the long summer evenings, just sitting in the glider on the front porch of her parents' house, listening to the soft churring of the insects and watching the moon. It was a forty-five minute buggy ride from the Trial farm to the Chavet place, but George was happy to make the trip.

On the first day of July, 1934, George married Virginia Chavet in her home town of Birmingham, Kansas. With the summer farm work that needed to be done they took no honeymoon, and in any case, cash was short in the years of the Great Depression. George told Virginia they'd take a trip in the winter, maybe to Florida. They moved in with Grace on the farm in Muscotah. That summer George was ecstatically happy. But his relationship with Virginia quickly soured.

By the summer of 1935, they spent as little time with each other as they could. She moved back to her parents' house, and by the spring of 1936 George had not seen Virginia for nearly six months. George hated to fail at anything, but, despite his intelligence and his education, he found he had nothing to say to Virginia. He wanted to talk about history and science and literature and all the adventure that waited for them far away from the prairie, but she only wanted to talk about small town society.

In the years ahead, he thought often of the afternoon she had moved back to her parents' house.

But, except for a tense meeting in the attorney's office when their divorce was finalized in 1939, he never saw Virginia again and never discussed her with anyone. That part of his life was over.

George spent the next year just working the farm, keeping to himself. He stopped going with his mother to church. Mostly he enjoyed working the fields by himself. Sometimes on hot summer afternoons, pitching hay into the loft, he'd take a break and stand in the shade looking out, and think about his future.

In July, 1936, he took a day off from work, put on his one suit, and rode to Atchison to contact Dr. Summerfield at St. Benedict's. He got there twenty minutes early for his nine o'clock appointment, so he strolled the familiar grounds and ended up at his favorite spot, the overlook.

"The University of Kansas City is a good school, George," Summerfield told him. "They're trying to grow their faculty, really make their medical program first-rate. I would be happy to write you a letter of recommendation."

"I'm not sure I want to be a doctor," George said. "I want to get a bachelor's degree, but I think I'd rather be a teacher than a doctor."

When he got back to Muscotah, he told his mother he was thinking about returning to school. She told him to do what he thought was best. As was his habit at the farm, he went up to the hayloft and stood gazing out thinking things through. The postmaster position had meant a lot to his father—the first step to a political career. George was well aware that the offer to fill out his father's term had been quite an honor for him. But he felt that suggesting he be a candidate for future terms was not really what the men in Atchison wanted, and that suited George just fine.

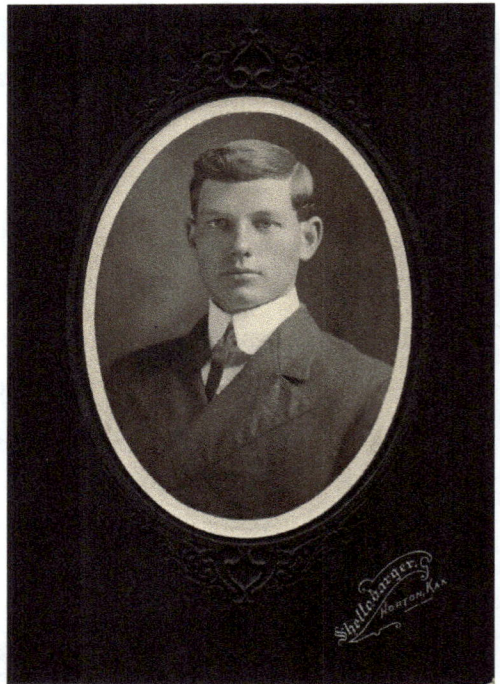

He thought often about his father and what had taken him from the handsome, confident young man to the tired man who'd put an end to his own life at age forty-seven.

That evening at the supper

table George told his mother he planned to apply to the University of Kansas City for the fall term, get a bachelor's degree, and maybe become a teacher.

"Not a doctor?" Grace asked.

"No," George said. "I've thought about it a good bit these last two years." He paused, moving his iced tea glass around the red checked table cloth. "I also want to travel."

"To where?" his mother asked, busy washing the dishes in a pan on the kitchen counter.

"I don't know yet. Everywhere."

After a long moment Grace said, "Well, education will help with that too. What you learn you'll always have with you."

George knew it would mean more work for his mother if he went back to school. "Elton has offered to sharecrop," he said.

"I know. I told him I'd let him know after you made up your mind." George smiled. She already knew what he was thinking and, in her practical way, had already planned how she could help him. Neither of them mentioned George's wife Virginia. Grace knew to leave that subject alone.

The next day George told the committee chair that he did not want to be considered for the postmaster position.

By August of 1933, Ruth had persuaded Mack and Juna that she needed to go to the University of Missouri in Columbia, a half-day train ride east of Kansas City.

"When I graduated from Kansas City Junior College last spring

I took the University entrance exam," Ruth said shyly. "The State of Missouri will soon be requiring all teachers to have a degree." They were standing on the narrow back porch that had become Mack's area. He came out here to smoke his pipe, and on mild days, he would sit in the rocking chair in the sun.

Juna and Mack exchanged glances and Mack said, "I guess we can afford it." A smile came over her face.

"But I want Bonnie to go there with you," Juna added. "To help you get settled in."

"The boarding house is at 401 Conley Lane," Ruth said eagerly. "Near campus, it's very nice…"

"Do they have a phone?"

"Yes. I copied down the number." Ruth handed it to her mother.

"I want you to call us every Sunday, after church," Juna said. "What's the lady's name?"

"Mrs. Westover," Ruth said, and she rushed off to tell Bonnie the good news.

Ruth walked with Bonnie the ten blocks to the Wabash train

station in Columbia. Sunday was clear and bright, the sky blue, clouds white. Ruth bubbled with enthusiasm. "Look at the flower beds. Just beautiful."

The street was quiet, but sunny and inviting with an atmosphere Ruth was coming to love. Garfield

Avenue back in Kansas City seemed much darker, with its old elm trees and its hills.

"Columbia's kind of like Nevada, isn't it?" Ruth chattered on. Bonnie seemed distracted. "I liked the big trees along Third Avenue. I liked the house on Central Avenue too. Remember?"

"That was a long time ago," Bonnie said quietly. They walked in silence for a moment.

"Only six years," Ruth said, caught up in the small town beauty of Columbia, oblivious to Bonnie's darker thoughts.

As Bonnie prepared to board the train for Kansas City, she put on her public persona—the vivacious beauty, the center of attention. Ruth waited until the train pulled away, walked back to her boarding house, and went up to her room. She opened the window a little and set her textbooks out neatly on her desk. Bonnie's literature book from Cottey College lay on the bed. Ruth put it back on the shelf and set to work on her homework for Monday.

In October, on a weekend when Bonnie was visiting, Ruth and Bonnie walked to Gaebler's for ice cream floats. A couple of the boys sitting at the counter were giving Bonnie the eye.

"Those boys are staring," Ruth whispered.

Bonnie snorted. "Ignore them."

"The boys are always interested in you," Ruth said. "I've never been as pretty as you are." She stopped, puzzled by the darkness in her sister's eyes. "I mean…I thought…" Ruth stumbled, trying to avoid the subject of marriage. Bonnie was already twenty-nine years old, past the age when most young women married. "I know you have to work to help take care of dad and mother."

"Mother's off with that church group of hers most of the time. She should be helping dad. As it is, I have to help him, and everything else in that house."

Ruth wished she'd never brought the subject up. "Mother's church is helping her…"

"Well, it's not helping me," Bonnie snapped. "Never has, never will."

Ruth was shocked. Bonnie put down her spoon and turned her brilliant smile on her sister. She touched Ruth's hand. "Don't worry. I'm just blowing off steam."

Ruth and Bonnie walked to Wabash station and waited for Bonnie's train to Kansas City. After the train had departed, Ruth walked back to the University and spent an hour strolling the quiet residential streets adjoining the campus. She envisioned herself living in a house there, with a husband, maybe two children. She thought of the notation on the photo she had found in her mother's book about being "happier than I ever expected to be…" and Ruth felt certain she would be too. No matter where I live, or what happens, she thought, I

can be happy.

On the hot summer morning of June 5, 1935, Ruth graduated from the University of Missouri. Her parents, sweltering in their Sunday clothes, came to Columbia to watch her accept her diploma, then they all walked downtown, ate lunch, and rode the train back to Kansas City. Ruth now had a Bachelor of Science degree in Education, with a major in physical education and a certificate to teach.

When she moved back into her old room at home, it seemed much smaller than she remembered. Her mother and father and sister seemed different too. During the evenings Juna would get down her bible and read from it, sometimes out loud. Ruth touched the other dusty books on the shelf, books she remembered from the house on Central Avenue in Nevada. She remembered the afternoon she and Bonnie had opened those books and seen her mother's girlish notes. Ruth pretended to look at the books while secretively casting a glance at her mother sitting in her chair under the reading lamp. She could not envision the girl who had made those notes. It all seemed so long ago.

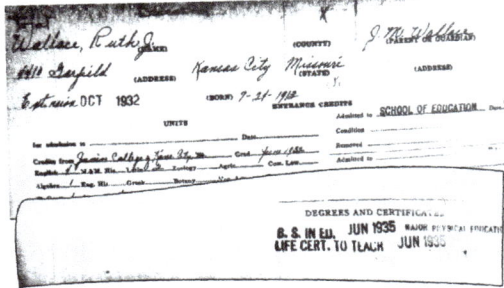

That summer Ruth landed a teaching position at the A. Louis Ruhl School at 63rd and Main. In September she began teaching home economics and girl's gym. Her new duties kept her fully occupied—riding the streetcar to school, teaching, preparing lessons in the evening. Her family's life went on as it had—her father a silent figure, her mother busy with church activities, Bonnie in her basement refuge. Ruth had no time to spare, but she had always been an obedient child, so when her mother asked her to, she would sit with her as she read her bible while Mack sat reading the newspaper. She knew it would give Bonnie more time to herself.

"Don't let her convert you," Bonnie said from behind a veil of Chesterfield smoke when Ruth came downstairs after a session with Juna. They had been reading the book of Matthew.

"She wants you and me to spend more time at church with her," Ruth said.

Bonnie snorted. "No thanks."

Ruth said nothing. In the dim light of the basement, the familiar trunks and stacked wooden chairs from the house in Nevada were the same as they had been for years. Ruth saw that the future had become elusive for her older sister. The bright promise that had always been in those dark and flashing eyes was fading. Confidence was becoming resignation. Frightened by what she saw, Ruth retreated upstairs.

In September, 1936, George moved into a room in a boarding house on Rockhill Road in Kansas City and began classes at the

University, majoring in biology. He immersed himself in his studies the same way he had immersed himself in farm work after his father's death. Two years went by in a flash. His grades were good, but undistinguished. By May 28, 1938, he had completed his course of study and was to be awarded a bachelor's degree in Biology.

The Curators of the
University of Missouri

To all whom it may concern, Greeting:

Be it known that the Curators, having been advised by the Faculty that

George T. Trial

has completed at the

University of Missouri at Kansas City

the course of study required of candidates for the degree of

Bachelor of Arts

Biology

and is qualified to receive the same, do by these presents confer said degree upon him with all honors and privileges appertaining thereto.

In testimony whereof the signatures of the proper officials and the seal of the University are affixed.

Done at the University of Missouri at Kansas City, State of Missouri

Replacement for diploma issued in the year of our Lord

one thousand nine hundred and thirty-eight

President, Board of Curators

Chancellor, University of Missouri at Kansas City

President, University of Missouri

Dean

He met his mother at the Kansas City train station the day of his graduation. She was dressed in her gray dress with the silver tassels— George recognized it as her one "good" outfit. He noticed she had stopped in Atchison and had her hair done. He felt a surge of pride in her.

After the ceremony they walked down the hill and across the Brush Creek Bridge to the Plaza and had ice cream at Wayand's. The afternoon seemed unreal. Grace worried about missing her train back to Muscotah, and George felt disoriented seeing his mother dressed in her church clothes walking with him along the sidewalks of the Plaza.

"Should we start for the station now?" Grace fretted.

George shook his head and spooned up the last of his vanilla ice cream. He had a real sweet tooth and his waistline was starting to show it. "We'll take a taxi. It's over a mile to walk."

"Mile's not so bad," Grace said.

He smiled. "You'll be back in plenty of time to change clothes and get the evening milking done. I'll be there day after tomorrow to help Elton get the hay cut and raked."

After his mother's train had left, he walked back to the Plaza and sat on the patio in back of the KC Grill smoking a cigar. My mother has never complained, he said to himself; not about anything that has happened to her, or about anything I've ever wanted to do, even marrying Virginia. Once I find a job I'm going to save enough money to get my divorce finalized.

He fanned himself with his hat. He'd graduated. He'd helped his mother sell the big Muscotah farm and buy a much smaller farm ten miles away at the edge of the tiny town of Effingham. The depression was ending and people had more cash now. She had some money in the bank and her needs were simple.

The breezy summer afternoon had deepened into evening and the air was cooling. People strolling by seemed happy and prosperous. Maybe the New Deal really was working. President Roosevelt had told them so often and for so long that happy days were here again that perhaps they had begun to believe him.

Over the tops of the buildings to the west, the summer clouds were turning peach in the evening light and it seemed like the whole wide world lay open to him.

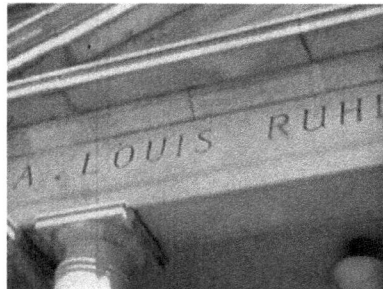

George kept his stuffy room in the boarding house on Rockhill Road while he began making applications for a teaching position in Kansas City. In July he received an offer to become a math and science teacher for the fifth and sixth grade at A. Louis Ruhl School at 63rd and Main.

Chapter 5

Ruth often passed George in the halls between classes at Ruhl School. He was a well-dressed young man, stocky, his thick hair always neatly combed. He introduced himself to her one day at lunch break. All through college, he had been called Talbert, his middle name, but now he introduced himself as George Trial.

They started meeting at lunch break while Ruth was outside supervising the kids at recess. Ruth thought he was articulate, energetic, and, like her, a dreamer. He was a sharp dresser, and a talker, but she liked his farm-bred manners; he opened doors for her. Eventually he asked her for a date and she agreed.

Saturday afternoon came. George had ridden the bus to the Plaza, then taken the Troost streetcar up to the 44th street stop.

He wore his gray double-breasted suit. It was almost seven in the evening, but the day was just beginning to cool. George was perspiring as he hurried down the sidewalk with a bouquet of flowers in hand. He was almost late and he hated being late.

He finally found the house—a gray one-story cottage with a porch and glider. He climbed the steps to the door and pressed the doorbell. Almost immediately the door opened to reveal a beautiful woman. He stepped back, flustered.

"You must be George," she said.

"Am I late?" he asked, embarrassed even at the thought.

"Not quite." Bonnie gave him a brilliant smile. "Come in."

He stepped into the small living room and saw Ruth dressed in a green dress, obviously new, coming out of the dining room. She smiled shyly.

George and Ruth began seeing each other every weekend. George was always nattily dressed, his hair combed straight back and parted in the middle like the Arrow shirt advertisements in Esquire magazine.

When the sultry days of August came, they went swimming at the Kansas City Country Club. George had never learned to swim, so he was not very enthusiastic about this.

Still, he enjoyed seeing Ruth in her black bathing suit. She was an athletic swimmer.

George began going to Oak Park Christian Church with Ruth and her mother, but he and Ruth never discussed religion. The moralizing, rigid sermons of Reverend Briney were not uplifting to either of them. Spirituality was not to be found in a sweltering church, but out in the great wide world, or in the quiet of a garden. George liked talking about the bible as history—the swirl of empires and peoples of the Middle East over the ages. About once a month they went to the Pla-Mor Ballroom at 3100 Main Street. Artie Shaw played there sometimes, and Tommy Dorsey. George and Ruth enjoyed dancing, even though he they weren't very good at it.

Ruth worried about her sister. She would sometimes creep down the stairs Saturday afternoon before she went out with George. Bonnie would be there, sitting in the old armchair she kept by the furnace, dreaming and smoking in the wan light. Her mother didn't allow smoking in the house, not even Mack's pipe, so Bonnie maintained the fiction by smoking her cigarettes in the basement, and Juna pretended not to know about it. All the fashionable women in the ice cream parlors and the shops smoked cigarettes, and Bonnie was very fashionable. On Saturday nights at the Pla-Mor there was always a solid haze of smoke in the room, but Ruth had never taken it up. "I guess I'm afraid I'll make myself look foolish," she had told George.

Now she just sat and looked at Bonnie, not knowing what to say.

"You've always been a dreamer," Bonnie told Ruth with more than a touch of irritation in her voice. "Back in the old house in Nevada, you were always sitting in the rocking chairs on the front porch or under the elm tree in the back yard, reading your books, daydreaming, mooning around by yourself."

"What's wrong with that?" Ruth asked. "You do it now."

"Well, it won't get you anywhere." Bonnie bantered.

Ruth shrugged; she knew she could never win an argument with her older sister. "George and I spend hours talking about history and geography and foreign travel."

"I wouldn't travel to Europe now," Bonnie retorted. "Hitler's army invaded western Poland yesterday."

Bonnie suddenly peered closer at Ruth. Ruth had never been able to lie to her or conceal what she felt, and a happy guilt was lurking behind Ruth's bland expression now.

"He asked you, didn't he?" Bonnie stated.

Ruth's eyes darted around the gloomy basement, but there was no place to hide.

"Not yet, but I'm sure he will soon, and I'm going to say yes."

The sisters were silent in the pale light. Bonnie's expression deepened; she stared hard at the asbestos cover on the old round ducts from the furnace. She forced her face to relax.

Ruth studied the four extra dining room chairs stored in the basement since they'd moved from the bigger house in Nevada. Bonnie shook a Chesterfield out of the pack and lit it. Their eyes met, and they both knew something had already changed between them. Some part of who they had been together had gone out of their lives and would never return. Ruth remembered the farm days at Sandstone, when she and her brother would follow Bonnie around, doing whatever she told them to do. Then Bonnie turned on her brilliant smile and said, "I'm happy for you." And everything seemed alright again.

Relief flooded Ruth's face. "I'm sorry. I know sisters should marry in order, but..."

Bonnie laughed out loud. "That's nonsense. Does father know yet, or mother?"

"Nobody knows yet, not even George. Only you." Ruth searched Bonnie's face. "Do you still think he's just a dreamer, overdressed and aimless?"

Bonnie smiled again. "Aimless, no, overdressed, yes. A dreamer, yes. But you're a dreamer too." She paused. "I heard mother say she thinks he's just a young man from a Kansas farm without much of a future, despite his snappy clothes. Just a teacher in an elementary school."

Ruth flushed. "Well, that's all I am, too, so why be so critical?"

Bonnie blew smoke at the dusty floor joists overhead. "I'm happy for you."

Ruth went up the stairs, ecstatic.

On a perfect spring Sunday in Swope Park, George spotted Ruth sitting on a plaid blanket under an elm tree. He tried to come up

silently, but she heard him coming and closed her book. She made room for him on the blanket. He sat down, touched her hand, and unbuttoned his double-breasted suit jacket. He was disappointed to see she was not reading the book he had given her the weekend before, *Drifter's Gold*.

"What are you reading?"

Ruth showed him the volume. "*Look Homeward, Angel.*" It had a Plaza Library stamp on the bottom.

He smiled at her. "You know, you look a little like Bette Davis."

She blushed. "Not Jean Harlow?" She primped her hair. "I could have it bleached platinum blonde. She's from Kansas City, you know."

George quickly changed the subject. They talked about their fellow teachers for a while, then started speculating about the future.

"Where will you be in twenty or thirty years? Principal?" Ruth asked.

"I'll be traveling the world."

"Europe is becoming a dangerous place, according to the articles I read in The Kansas City Star." Ruth laid a hand on George's arm. She had long elegant fingers, nails painted scarlet.

George took her hand. "You have beautiful hands," he told her. "I think your left hand will be even more beautiful with this." He took a small purple velvet box out of his pocket and gave it to her. "Will you marry me?"

Inside the box was a modest engagement ring. Smiling, Ruth looked up at George and said, "Yes."

In late August, 1939, the tensions in Europe had pushed even Tom Pendergast's shenanigans off the front page of the newspaper. The Third Reich had absorbed most of Austria and Czechoslovakia. The Empire of the Rising Sun now claimed Manchuria. In Kansas City people talked endlessly about war, but no one seemed to have a clear idea of what needed to be done. In Washington there was talk of instituting a draft. General Marshall was preparing a confidential briefing for President Roosevelt asking for authority to fire forty percent of the army general officers and start recruitment of a new million man army.

Ruth and George spent lazy days window-shopping on the Plaza, watching movies at the theater, and having picnics in Swope Park. They played tennis on summer mornings before it got too hot, and went to the pool at the country club on top of the hill behind the Plaza.

George made three trips to his mother's farm in the summer of 1939 to help with farm work. He spent three days each time, pining for Ruth, but getting his work done too. He got the old sickle bar hay reaper fixed, cut the hay, and raked it.

One day he went up the ladder into the hayloft to repair some of the boards in the floor that were getting loose. Driving nails into the age-hardened oak planks was difficult. He bent a lot of nails. After an hour he sat on the loft end, door open to the hot summer wind rich with the smell of cut alfalfa, the July heat bending the air above the green pasture. Beyond the tree line the sky was a hazy blue.

He leaned out a little, looking west. The few clouds in the west might mean some rain tonight or tomorrow. Thoughts passed slowly across his mind. He realized with certainty that he would never be a doctor. He felt less regret than he expected. He and Ruth were taking an education course this summer, polishing their teaching skills. He could get a master's degree and start angling for the principal's job sometime down the line, but he wasn't certain he wanted that.

In his mind's eye he was back at St. Benedict's again, looking out past the river to the flat prairie. He felt the breeze rolling in from miles of flatlands, rising up the bluffs by the river. He strained forward, looking and listening for something from far away, past the edge of the pasture where the trees bent in the wind. But what? It was only the fencerow of a cow pasture on a small farm in Kansas. After a while he picked up his tools—the hammer and nail apron that had been his father's—and went back to work.

On the train back to Kansas City, George stared out the window at the familiar landscape flashing by; but he saw far beyond, to all the unknown lands of the great world.

He'd bought wedding rings from Helzberg Jewelers on the Plaza, and now he pulled the box out of his jacket pocket and looked at the polished gold bands. Ruth and I will be married for the rest of our lives, he promised himself.

The wedding was May 20, 1940, in Oak Park Christian Church.

At the wedding, Grace, ill at ease in the big city and among strangers, stayed close to Uncle Walter, who had a lively conversation with Ruth's brother Jack, both of them railroad men. After the ceremony, people spilled out of the stifling church and the wedding party rode the street car back to the Wallace house, where they sat on the front porch drinking lemonade and fanning themselves.

CERTIFIED COPY
MARRIAGE LICENSE
No. A 78766
OFFICE OF
RECORDER OF DEEDS
Jackson County, Missouri
At Kansas City

STATE OF MISSOURI, } ss.
County of Jackson

This License authorizes any Judge, Justice of the Peace, licensed or ordained Preacher of the Gospel, who is a citizen of the United States, or other person authorized under the laws of this State to solemnize marriage between George Trial of the County of Jackson and State of Missouri who is over the age of twenty-one years and Ruth Wallace of the County of Jackson and State of Missouri who is over the age of eighteen years.

Witness my hand as Recorder, with the seal of office hereto affixed, at my office in Kansas City, Missouri, this 16 day of May 19 40
(L.S.) JOHN P. SHERROD RECORDER.
By J.A. Kilmer DEPUTY RECORDER.

STATE OF MISSOURI, } ss.
County of Jackson

This is to certify that the undersigned, a Minister of the Gospel did, in said County and State at the 20 day of May A. D. 19 40 unite in marriage the above named persons.
Russell R Briney, Pastor
Oak Park Christian church, K.C. Mo.

Filed for record and duly recorded in my office this 21 day of May A. D. 19 40
JOHN P. SHERROD Recorder. By J.A. Kilmer DEPUTY RECORDER.

CERTIFICATE
STATE OF MISSOURI, } ss.
County of Jackson

I, JOHN P. SHERROD, Recorder of Deeds, within and for the County of Jackson, aforesaid, do hereby certify that the above and foregoing is a full, true and complete copy of the Marriage License and Certificate of Marriage of said parties as the same appears of record in my office in Book 150 Page 550
IN TESTIMONY WHEREOF, I hereunto set my hand and affix the official seal of said office, at Kansas City, Missouri, this 7 day of June A. D. 194 6
JOHN P. SHERROD, Recorder.
By M. Brandmeyer DEPUTY RECORDER

(SEAL)
Form 1—Kansas City Marriage Lic. Cert. Copy—630—3-46

The couple had decided on a honeymoon trip to California. "We'll take the train to Los Angeles," George said. He had kept his suit jacket on and his tie knotted, even though he was mopping sweat off his forehead.

"For land's sake, Talbert, take your jacket off. It's soaked," Grace said quietly to George.

He slipped his jacket off and she hung it on the wood coat rack behind the door where he later forgot it and had to walk back three blocks to retrieve it.

Ruth and George boarded the train for their honeymoon in California the next morning. They stayed at the Mar Vista hotel in

Santa Monica and walked the gardens in the cool ocean breeze. They strolled through the park overlooking the pier and let the sea breeze cool them. The sun-dappled grass was beautiful, with flowers everywhere.

"I could live here," George told Ruth. "Business is booming; there's oil, the railroads, the shipping industry. They even make airplanes here, just like in Wichita."

"Why not get into the movies?" Ruth laughed. "There's Hollywood over there." She pointed past the pier toward the groves between Santa Monica and Los Angeles. He hugged her.

"What's that down there, the big Arabian Nights-looking building at the base of the pier?" she asked.

They learned that the ornate building was called the La Monica Ballroom—the biggest and best ballroom on the West Coast.

"It's Tommy Dorsey tonight," Ruth said, reading the marquee. "I love his song 'Talk Slow.'"

George studied the ads beside the door. "Opens at six o'clock, cover charge one dollar," he read. "Holds up to five hundred people. Wow!"

"Can we go tonight?"

"Sure," he said. "But we probably won't know the dances they do here on the West Coast."

"Back at the Pla-Mor, you used to tell me you did the foxtrot to every song since that's the only dance you knew."

"Still true," he said. "Makes me a very versatile dancer. Probably why you married me, I'll bet."

"Not at all," Ruth laughed. "It was your family fortune."

When they returned to Kansas City ten days later, Jack met them at Union Station.

"You two look like an old married couple." He grinned. Collecting their suitcases for them, he tipped the red-cap a quarter.

On Sunday August 29, 1940, Ruth and George were at their usual spot in Swope Park. It was cool under the trees. Earlier that morning, they had attended the ten-thirty service at Oak Park Christian Church with Juna, Mack, and Bonnie. Now they were spending a quiet Sunday afternoon in Swope Park, sitting on their usual plaid blanket in the shade of an oak tree and picnicking on ham sandwiches, boiled eggs, and lemonade. George was reading The Kansas City Star, but he put it down slowly and gazed at Ruth.

"I'll be thirty next December," he said solemnly. Ruth wondered where this conversation might go, but she kept a smile on her face.

He stared at the folded newspaper. "General Marshall is testifying to Congress that we need to mobilize five hundred thousand men immediately." He pushed the newspaper across to her. The headline read, "Draft Bill Passed."

"You want to join the army," Ruth said finally.

"They won't take anyone over thirty years old. I'm twenty-nine."

George watched her looking up past the oak and elm trees toward the long sweep of lawn in front of the Nelson Art Gallery.

"I think you should do what you want to do," she said so softly he could barely hear.

"After I finish the basic officer's course, we can get married quarters at whatever base I get assigned to."

She smiled. "Alright."

He felt a great flood of tension flow out of him. Tension he had not even known was there.

George was sworn in as a second lieutenant at Fort Leavenworth, Kansas on September 14, 1940. After two months of officer basic training at Fort Leavenworth, he was given his 'branch' assignment—the Army Quartermaster Corps—an unglamorous assignment which he set about trying to convince himself was a good assignment. In 1941, the U.S. Army still required its officers, in all branches, to be skilled riders. George excelled at this since he'd enjoyed riding from his boyhood on the farm.

His next assignment was to Fort Riley, Kansas. He was given married quarters housing—a one bedroom apartment in a three story brick barracks shaded by cottonwood trees. Ruth came to join him.

At first George worried that Ruth would hate living on an army base, not knowing anyone. But he was delighted to find she had

an easy adaptability and quickly made their Spartan apartment into a home. She amused herself, housekeeping and reading and walking during the day. She made friends with her neighbors quickly and, instead of complaining, pointed out the nice features of their new home—the thick walls of the building stayed cool even in the prairie heat. They went to the officers' club and Ruth quickly grasped the basics of being a junior officer's wife—to socialize with the other wives, but to always remember the hierarchy of rank that was even more stringent for wives than for husbands. George was immensely proud.

One evening he and Ruth went for a walk down the long gravel path alongside the training field. The sun was setting and the hot breath of the prairie wind was sighing away to silence. The evening star was bright in a royal blue sky.

"The clean dry scent of the prairie reminds me of home," George said. "I used to ride in a horse-drawn buggy with my father. He'd pick me up after school and we'd ride to the post office together— he was postmaster in our town. He'd finish his work while I stayed in Wehmeyer's general store next door, exploring all the supplies on the shelves—nails and tools, harness leather, rolls of gingham. I can remember the smell of it even now." He glanced at her. "Silly isn't it?"

"No. You so seldom speak of the past, I often wonder..."

"Not much to tell. My father died while I was at college in Atchison back in 1933. He killed himself."

Ruth was silent for a moment, then took his hand. "It must have been difficult."

"Harder on my mother than on me, but she did not complain."

"I like her," Ruth said. "She has that ability to accept things, good or bad, and never lose her enthusiasm for life."

"You have that too," George said. They walked in silence back to their apartment.

A few weeks later they paid a visit to Grace at her new farm, twenty acres on the edge of the tiny town of Effingham, Kansas.

Ruth enjoyed helping Grace pick blackberries and make a pie.

"George loves pies," Grace confided. She was beginning to like this tall quiet girl from Kansas City.

In autumn, George was transferred to Fort Campbell, Kentucky in early spring for five months training. He applied for a transfer from the Quartermaster Corps to the Army Air Corps and was accepted.

89

Sitting in their apartment one evening George said to Ruth, "You seem to be doing fine with all this moving, having to meet a new set of people, be in a new place. Are you alright with it really?"

She smiled. Yes."

"One more move, George told her. Minter Field, Texas.

Ruth's days were easy enough while George was attending flight school. And she had no difficulty with the many required social interactions young army officers and their wives were required to participate in. She was a modest and unassuming young woman. Her good manners and the way she made the most of her limited wardrobe made her popular among the wives. She had learned as a child how to be her own person while Bonnie was taking the lead in all things. Now that ability to be fully self-contained, yet fully engaged with her companions, was a major asset. She and George had no social connections, no educational pedigree, so they were saved the pressure of snobbery that was rife in the rapidly growing army. They felt no need to try to get ahead with more than fair play and hard work.

After an evening at the officers' club they'd often have a good laugh over the antics of George's fellow officers who were ferociously ambitious. Everybody knew war was coming and they were in a hurry to maximize the promotion potential that this entailed. Ruth's willingness to listen was a major asset among the junior officers and their wives, whose conversations were usually designed for professional advancement.

"Thanks," George told her one night after a particularly grueling evening at the monthly officers' club 'hail and farewell.'

Ruth laughed. "It's not difficult. Those people need their rank and their status, promotions and authority, to be who they are. We don't."

"And you are okay living in military housing?"

"Of course," she said. "One day, though, let's have a house of our own."

"I promise we will," George said.

They were home on leave at Ruth's parents' house on Garfield Avenue the first week of December, 1941. A thick blanket of snow had fallen Saturday night, but the sun was out Sunday morning when the family walked the four blocks to church for the 10:30 service. After a big midday dinner, George and Mack sat in the living room reading through The Kansas City Star while the women cleaned the dishes.

"Want to walk down to the Plaza?" George asked Ruth when she joined them in the living room.

Ruth got her coat and they walked to the Paseo, then to 46th street, past the Nelson Art Gallery, and to the Plaza. They strolled past the shops on the Plaza until nearly four o'clock, then started home.

"What a beautiful snowy day," Ruth said. "So quiet. So peaceful." The sky was a deep clear blue. The streets were silent; not a single car passed them all the way home.

Inside the house, Mack, Juna, and Bonnie were clustered around the radio Mack had moved to the dining room table. He sat with his hand on the dial making minute adjustments. An announcer was saying something in excited tones.

"What?" George said.

Juna shushed him.

"…as we have been told, the president will address the nation tomorrow. For now, all we know is that several hours ago, there was an attack on the American fleet in the Hawaiian Islands."

Ruth and George stared at each other. George brought two more chairs and they joined their family in a circle around the table, staring at the radio. After a while, President Roosevelt's message was repeated. George went into the other room and put on his uniform. He tried to call Fort Leavenworth from the phone on the wall in the hallway, but the lines were jammed. "I need to get to the base," he said.

Mack put his hand on George's arm. "The last train north has already left. Better stay here tonight, try to get back to the base first thing in the morning."

He and Ruth lay together on the roll-away bed in the living room. They couldn't sleep. They whispered into the night about what might happen, about what they should do.

Monday morning, Juna had the radio going early. After breakfast, when George and Ruth were washing and drying dishes, they heard Juna call, "The President's on the radio speaking to Congress!"

They rushed into the other room. "Since Sunday, a state of war has existed between the United States and the Empire of Japan," President Roosevelt told a stunned nation.

George and Ruth stood staring at each other in the middle of the familiar living room that suddenly didn't seem familiar at all.

Chapter 6

After finishing the B-17 flight engineer course at Minter Field, Texas, George was given his assignment—Keflavik Airfield, Iceland, the mid-Atlantic refueling and repair base for the hundreds of bombers being ferried to Britain from the United States.

George arrived in a B-17 in March, 1942, and found, to his surprise, that the weather was warmer than it had been in Boston, where he'd waited four days for a ride. He quickly settled into the office routine, which was to coordinate the business of planes, fuel, and supplies being shipped to Britain. George had always been highly organized, so managing the steady stream of planes and the mountains of supplies and parts they carried was not difficult once he got a system in place. He expected to be there no more than a few months, but it was over two years before he was reassigned to the 91st Bomb Wing in England.

He had the capable help of a number of Icelanders who were fluent in English and highly educated. They were in fact professors from the University of Iceland, volunteered to the U.S. base. They were happy to talk about their country.

At the time, Iceland's economy was centered on cod fishing and sheep herding. The entire population of the country was less than two hundred thousand, smaller than Kansas City. Iceland was a colony of Denmark, although the island had been electing its own governing officials since 1900. After the Nazis occupied Denmark, Iceland had been left entirely on its own.

The other Americans in his detachment had little interest in

Iceland aside from Saturday night in the bars of Reykjavik. They spent their spare time playing poker in the barracks. But George was happy to have Kristmann Gundmundsson and Helgi Tryggvason educate him on Iceland's culture. "After all, we are professors," Gundmundsson joked.

Gas rationing forced them to make their sightseeing excursions on foot. George was shown the hot springs, shimmering aquamarine pools steaming in the clear air. They walked to a lava field one Saturday. It was all quite interesting, but for George, hiking felt a lot like farm work.

Most weekends after breakfast in the mess hall, he walked the mile to Reykjavik and spent mornings wandering the streets, soaking up the colors. At ten in the morning it was still the deep blue of dawn. He would walk down Tjarnargata Street along the lake, down cobbled streets past houses and buildings with corrugated steel siding painted

red and blue and green and yellow. If the day was mild, he would sit on a bench watching the kids ice skating on the lake. He usually stopped in one of the small cafés for a cup of tea and a scone. His professors would meet him there and they would continue their discussion of Icelandic history and culture.

Icelandic was a language little changed from the days of the Vikings, when all the North Atlantic countries spoke the same Old Norse language. George watched steam rising from his tea and listened to the soft roll of the Icelandic language around him. For George it was like having the best private tutors imaginable.

Later they might go the university library or the city archives and look at some of the original sagas kept there. The volumes were elegantly hand-lettered in Latin on vellum.

"They were actually written several hundred years after the

events they describe," Kristmann explained.

George hadn't thought of the Vikings as being lovers of history and language, but he found that they were. The sagas, originally oral records passed down from generation to generation, then copied down in the twelfth century, told stories as compelling as any current events.

Helgi shyly produced a book. "Heimskringla, one of the sagas."

"It's in English," Kristmann added.

George thanked them profusely and over the next few weeks

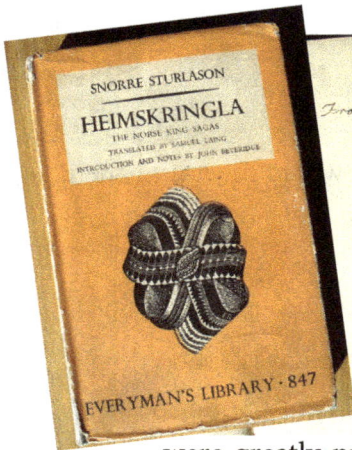

read it cover to cover. The Viking culture was democratic and aggressively expansionist, founded on farming and cattle raising. Women were respected, and tool-making, arts and crafts, and story-telling were greatly prized. Honor and fair dealing between the extended families that owned the land was the bedrock of Viking culture. These were the same qualities he knew from the prairie farms of Kansas. In his mind's eye, he saw the sunny campus at St. Benedict's college, his favorite spot overlooking the Missouri River and the prairies.

The world is a big and fascinating place, George mused. I like teaching, but I don't want to go back to teaching sixth graders at the Ruhl School in Kansas City. He sipped his tea. He knew he would be transferred to England eventually, so he felt he should take advantage of this leisurely assignment.

'Doctor Trial,' Kristmann and Helgi called him, and he would grin self-consciously. But he liked the sound of it. My thesis would be history, obviously, he thought. I won't have time to complete it while I'm here, but I could write a Master's level thesis. I don't want to write another pointless study of some obscure and forgotten literary figure of the eighteenth century, based on other people's writings.

"Shall we return to…?" Kristmann said politely, interrupting George's thoughts.

George stood and paid for all of them with military scrip. They made their way out into the early dusk. "Let's walk to the lake, shall we?" George suggested.

They stood watching until the last kids removed their skates and left for home.

"I'd like to ask your help," George began carefully.

"Certainly," they replied in unison.

"I want to do some research on the Icelandic education system. As it is today."

Puzzled but affable, his two guides agreed to help, starting the next weekend.

George hurried home through the darkness, heedless of the eerie green glow of the northern lights overhead. In the barracks he brushed past four tables of poker players under a haze of cigar smoke.

"Why don't you join us, George," Wally called after him. "We need your money." But George ignored them, still wrapped up in his idea. His book would be a survey of the history of the education system in Iceland. He began making notes that night.

Every weekend Helgi and Kristmann and their colleagues took George to one part or another of the Icelandic education system. He took extensive notes and in the evening struggled to condense them into a meaningful narrative. He was struck by how similar the kids were to the kids he had known back in Kansas City. Regardless of war raging across the world, kids will still play jump rope and smile when their picture is taken.

When he became bogged down in his project, George would sometimes walk up to the top of the hill overlooking the airfield to admire the view and breathe the clear, fresh air. He would sit on the rocks and look at the flat ocean, the city of Reykjavik to his right, the mountains beyond the bay.

A formation of B-17s slanted down toward the airfield, but George's mind was on the Viking sagas in the museum—the straightforward accounts of exploration, fighting, farming. Stories of sailing beyond the horizon and making a life in places never seen before by man. What must they have felt, to leave family and familiar farms behind and set sail for an unknown land, an unknown future?

The day turned chill as clouds came up from the bay. George got up and started down the hill, restless thoughts in his head. He was nearly finished with his thesis and thoughts of travel were in his mind. Before the army I travelled a bit, he thought, to Florida and to the Dakota gold fields. Now I've come halfway across the Atlantic, and soon I'll be in England.

When this war is over I want to go farther yet—across Asia, across the Pacific, around the world. A flight of four B-17s lifted off and circled east for England and the war with Germany. George found himself walking faster as he mused, "I want to make something of myself. I'm already thirty-three years old."

As he tramped down the hill toward the barracks under the clear points of stars, his thoughts drifted to a time long past in Muscotah, back when he was a young boy.

One night at the dining room table in Muscotah after dinner, as was her habit, his mother turned the kerosene lamps down to conserve fuel. The glow from behind the glass in the coal stove lit the room a soft yellow-red. Lloyd always wore a suit when he went to the post office and he still had it on, tie loosened.

"Lots of things come and go, Talbert," he said slowly. "I've learned that."

Ten-year-old George was puzzled by the darkness that came into his father's eyes from time to time.

"Some men spend their lives chasing after something…" He let the words trail off, then got up and poured himself the last of the coffee. "Searching for something that may not exist." He looked at George. "I've met a lot of people, son. I know a little bit about human nature. Some men, good men, work their whole lives and end up with nothing."

He shot young George a look, then softened it with a wan smile. "Don't worry; you're not like that. You'll do fine. And the way to do that is by educating yourself. There's a lot more to the world than

Atchison County, Kansas."

Grace touched Lloyd's shoulder. "I'm going to bed," she said. She went into the adjoining bedroom and swung the door most of the way closed, but not all the way; it would get too cold in the bedroom without some heat from the coal stove, the only heat in the house.

"When you're older I want you to go to college—St. Benedict's over in Atchison."

George was frowning, he didn't want to leave home. "I thought that was a church or a prison. It looks like one."

Lloyd smiled and tapped the boy's shoulder gently. "It used to be a monastery, but now it's a college too, and the best one around here. How about we go fishing at Perry Lake this Sunday afternoon?"

The boy brightened. "Yes, let's go."

George, lost in reminiscence, crunched through the ice up to the barracks door and into the cigar haze that wrapped the nightly poker games.

"Join us George, get out of the library and donate some of your money," Eddie said.

"Not tonight," laughed George as he returned to the present. "Got to work on my book."

As he completed each chapter he would mail the draft to Ruth and she would type it and mail it back to him. The huge airfield provided frequent and free mail service for George. The manuscript went to a publisher in Britain that the Icelandic professors had contacted and W. Heffer and Sons published the slim ninety-five page volume in 1944, just as George received his orders transferring him to active flight duty in England. His book included an acknowledgement of many of the Icelanders he had met during his two year stay—Jakob Kristinsson, director of public education; Freysteinn Gunnarson, headmaster of the teachers' training school; Soren Thoracius, headmaster of the largest of Iceland's three elementary schools. On his last day, Helgi and Kristmann each presented him with a signed copy of a book they had carefully chosen for him to commemorate their time together. George was overcome with emotion.

For the rest of his life George harbored thoughts of writing another book, but the years went by and he never did.

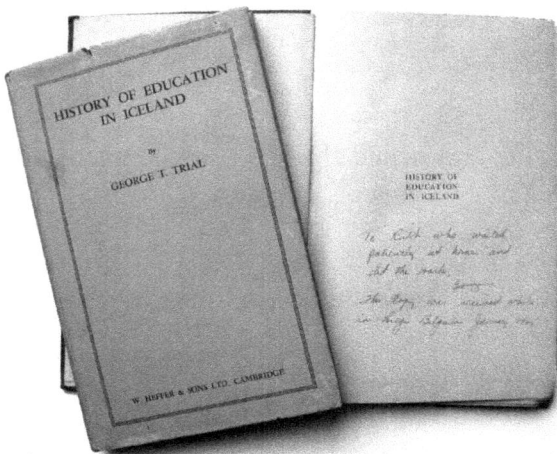

Years later he regretted not listing Ruth on the acknowledgements page of his book. After all, she had done all the typing and editing. Instead, he signed the first copy he received in 1945 to her, crediting her hard work.

When George transferred to England he was assigned to an Eighth Air Force B-17.

In the cold English fog he closed his mind to his fear and focused only on the daily routine. Every morning in the 4:00 a.m. cold he would walk through the mud from his Quonset hut to the briefing room. He would copy down the mission information, gulp down a half cup of bad coffee, then out to the tarmac for the preflight check of the plane.

He missed the warm café on Tjarnargata Street in Reykjavik where he had so recently enjoyed flavorful hot tea while he worked on his book and discussed history with the Icelanders. Those days seemed like a far away past.

But the missions that the American B-17s flew were safer now. The bombers were escorted by big North American P-51 fighters, with 400 MPH top speed, a 30,000 foot service ceiling, and eight fifty caliber machine guns.

In these fighters, the fresh young American pilots could easily outperform the fuel-starved Luftwaffe Me 109s they faced.

The deadly routine of bombing Germany into ruin continued. Planes were lost, but George never suffered a scratch. He closed his mind to the explosions in the German cities below him.

In late June 1944, soon after the D-Day invasion, George was reassigned to the 96th military intelligence battalion and transferred to a makeshift HQ in France. He was assigned a Jeep and a French driver-translator, and told to assess bomb damage in Normandy.

To the East the fighting continued, but in liberated Normandy, life was returning to normal.

As George rode past farms and villages in the mild summer sun, he thought of Ruth and the glamour photo of her that he carried, but he seldom got it out and looked at it. During the long hours in the cold air over Germany he had not dared think of the possibility that the future they planned together might never happen.

One afternoon, returning to their tiny 'headquarters' in the village of St. Marie du Mont, George noticed the door of the elementary school across the square was open to the mild afternoon. He heard children's voices and thought of him and Ruth teaching at Ruhl school.

He got a handful of Hershey bars out of the box he carried with him on his inspection trips and strolled across to the school.

When he appeared in the doorway, the dozen pupils and the young woman teacher froze. George waved the French translator over and asked him to explain that he would like to get her impressions of the fighting in the town the night of the D-Day invasion.

After a time the young lady relaxed a bit. The children still eyed George's uniform with fear, but their fear subsided as the teacher started talking to the translator. A thought occurred to George.

"Please ask her to have the kids write down their impressions of the night of the invasion."

George laid eight Hershey bars on a battered desk and all eyes turned to them. Here and there a shy smile appeared. Soon all the students were busy with pencils and crayons.

Marie Poulain
1r an.

Rédaction

Développement

Nous avons été très surpris de voir les Américains arrivés. Ce jour nous était inconnu; le 6 juin.

Le matin quand nous nous sommes levés, papa nous dit : Venez voir le matériel qui est arrivé dans la cour. Maman et moi suivîmes les conseils de papa, et nous allâmes voir dans la cour. Mais en regardant tout cela vous ne savez pas qu'est ce mot...

notre grand escalier et je priai. J'ai espéré que nos prisonniers reviendraient bientôt et que

les Américains gagneraient. Mais, j'espère toujours que les prisonniers vont bientôt revenir.

Quel jour que le 6 juin. Je n'aurais jamais cru que le débarquement se serait fait ici. À présent

de noir. Maman alla dans la salle et je la suivis. De partout on entendait rien que du bruit.

Dans la nuit qu'est ce que j'ai eu peur, les avions qui bombardaient la S.C. et allemande qui tirait sur les avions alliés, les fusils tiraient aussi, la mitrailleuse marchait, quelle vie d'enfer.

Je croyais bien mourir ce jour là, tellement que j'avais peur. Je faisais que de trembler, mon cœur battait fort. Je me disais, si les Allemands repoussent les Américains ils nous tueraient.

Chaque coup que ça bombardait mitraillait je me réfugiais dans

je suis bien heureuse, parce que les Américains nous ont délivrés de nos ennemis. Ils sont nos meilleurs amis.

"They will also make drawings," the translator said. "I will translate their words."

That evening, back in his room in the shell-pocked hotel, George filled out his official report. He started to write a line about the schoolkid's notes, but stopped.

As he looked at the drawings and read the translations he felt all his own fear from his days in B-17s rise up inside him and for a moment he could only sit silently until his tears subsided.

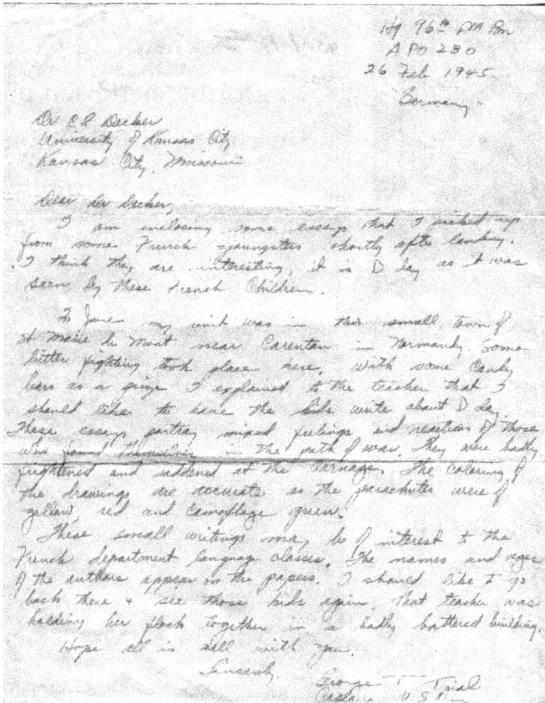

After carrying them around for over six months, George placed the essays and drawings in an envelope addressed to Dr. Decker at the university in Kansas City. He suggested the writings might be useful to the French language department, but in reality the gesture was his sentimental release of custody of what he held as a true and significant first hand account of D-Day by traumatized children in a war-torn countryside. These drawings were too precious to consign to a vast and impersonal military file.

For two years Bonnie and Ruth had spent ten hours a week at the Red Cross station set up in a tent in the parking lot of the Nelson Art Gallery. Bonnie had become her old self—full of purpose, crisp and confident in her starched Red Cross uniform. She'd been put in charge of four teams of women assembling medical packs for shipping to Europe.

Ruth was assigned to one of her teams. Bonnie and Ruth continued to teach school during the weekdays between their Red Cross duties. It was tiring, but it kept their minds occupied, and Ruth liked the way Bonnie had become her old self again—just like back in Nevada—confident and full of energy. Ruth was happy just to be a team member, assembling the little kits of bandages. She kept her mind off what the bandages might be used

for. On Sundays Ruth accompanied her mother to church and they prayed for George. Sometimes even Bonnie came along.

It was a bright May morning in 1945 when news came that Hitler was dead and Nazi Germany had surrendered. George wandered out of town and stared around at the countryside, lush with spring green. The other men from his unit were wandering aimlessly between the buildings. Bottles made the rounds, and the men shook hands with each other endlessly.

Soon new orders came through. All the flyable bombers were to be ferried across the Middle East, India, and Indonesia to continue the war with Japan.

George was transferred back to England and assigned to help inventory the hundreds of B-17s parked at air bases across Southern England.

There was an eerie ghostliness about the warplanes sitting empty in the pleasant English afternoon. George would swing up through the hatch behind the engineer's station and slide into the cockpit. He wasn't running a performance test, just confirming that all parts were there and the aircraft looked flight worthy.

He would then crawl back past the empty bomb racks and the silent machine guns still trailing their belts of ammo. Ghosts were there, specters of the fear and death that had been all around captured forever in the smell of spent cordite.

George did his work stolidly, thinking often of Ruth and when they would be together again. He wrote to her every day.

It was July before he received orders transferring him to Military Air Transport Command Logistics Center in Washington, D.C. He left three days later. Most of the Americans had left their quarters in disarray, ecstatic to be leaving Europe, the war, and the army behind as fast as they could. But George was an orderly and conscientious man. He packed his trunk and duffel bag and turned in his linen and towels to base supply, keeping one blanket for warmth in the cold interior of the B-17 that would bring him back across the North Atlantic. Then he swept out his cubicle and reported to the ready room for the four day trip back to the States.

As the formation of B-17s droned through the night, he sat in a torpor in the roaring cold, wrapped in his blanket like the rest of the passengers, thinking of all he'd seen and done in the last three years.

For the rest of his life he never spoke of his time with the Eighth Air Force in Europe.

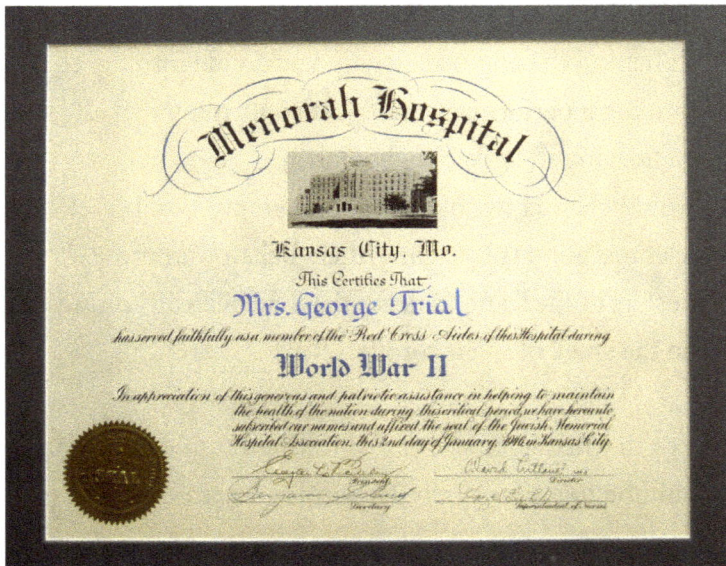

In Kansas City, the war over, the Red Cross tent was taken down, the team dismissed, and Bonnie and Ruth put their uniforms away. They received certificates for their service. Ruth put hers out on the mantel, but Bonnie did not, and after a few days Ruth took hers down too. The sooner the war was forgotten, the better.

Once again Bonnie would help Juna and Mack, then retire to her refuge in the basement to smoke Chesterfields, reading or listening to Ella Fitzgerald on the Victrola while Mack soaked up the sun on the back porch.

Chapter 7

Jack liked working in sales. He was a personable and outgoing man, and talking with clients and potential clients of the Great Northern Railroad was fun. Plus he liked the lakes and the cool pine forests of Minnesota and Wisconsin. Driving from town to town suited him too. He'd often daydream as he drove the long stretches of two-lane highway, sometimes of adventures patterned after the Edgar Rice Burroughs books he still read. His territory extended south to Omaha and included a stop in York, Nebraska, where Continental Grain Company was expanding its elevator operations. The manager there, James Crane, was not an easy man to deal with, and after a long afternoon dealing with Crane's short temper and overbearing ways, Jack would go to his hotel, change clothes, and go to the Tip Top diner. It was owned by the Gilmore family; their four daughters all waitressed there. The girls were tall and rangy, not particularly attractive, but cheerful,

GREAT FOR FREIGHT

smiling, and hard-working. The convivial atmosphere in the Tip Top was as refreshing as the draft Hamm's beer Jack drank with his steak and potato dinner.

The next morning before he got in his Plymouth to drive to the next stop, he would have breakfast at the Tip Top—two eggs over easy, ham, toast, and two cups of coffee. Jack always left a generous fifty-cent tip. He flirted with all the girls, but it was Doris he liked the best. And

she thought he was something special too, this laughing young man in his snappy suit and two-tone shoes.

Jack and Doris married on November 25, 1947, and moved into an apartment at 1700 North 21st Street in Superior, Wisconsin, where they lived the rest of their lives. When Jack's sales trips took him south to Kansas City, Doris would ride the train to York, visit with her family, then go on to Kansas City

113

for a day or two. Bonnie and Doris became good friends.

While Jack renewed old friendships with his buddies at the Kansas City Southern Railway, Doris would help Juna with the cleaning and ironing and cooking so Bonnie could have some time for herself.

Throughout their lives, Jack and Doris Wallace's apartment was a pleasant jumble of 'collectibles' of every description. Jack loved the outdoors—he and Doris played golf and fished most weekends—but he had no desire to travel just for travel's sake. He was a cheerful man, happy in his work, happy in his marriage, and happy with his motley collection of books, electrical insulators, coins, and stamps. Doris learned to paint in watercolor, and he enjoyed having her pictures out on the mantel.

Back from Europe and assigned to Military Air Transport Command in Washington, D.C., Major George Trial shared an office with Lieutenant Colonel Harry Snyder and Major Harry Sessums—three gray steel Army desks jammed into a twelve-by-fourteen foot room with one window overlooking the granite wall that was the back of the State Department building. He found an apartment in Georgetown, Ruth came East to join him, and they settled into a comfortable routine.

George and his colleagues spent their days making lists of planes and flight radiuses and refueling stock needs. But as the days passed, they found that the senior officers in Air Transport Command had little interest in their lists. The three of them spent most of their time with their feet up on their desks talking about the future. They were also assigned the task of helping demobilize the hundreds of thousands of men leaving the service. It was simple enough—get quadruplicate sets of demobilization orders for the day's list of men, go to the demob center (a warehouse on K Street), and oversee the long lines of men shuffling from one station to the next turning in gear and signing papers. The men only had to follow the yellow line painted on the floor, receive final pay at the last station, count it at the long table, sign for it, and then walk out the side door a civilian. George and the two Harrys took turns going to the demob station.

On weekends Ruth and George made sightseeing excursions around Washington, D.C., which had taken on an atmosphere of languor after the end of the war.

"I hope you're not bored," George said, straightening up and

115

hitching his pants. Ruth knew his uniform was too tight. He'd put on ten pounds since he'd come back from Europe, but he refused to buy new uniforms.

"I'm not," she said with a smile to mask her unease, "but I think you are."

He nodded. "This assignment is boring, but I'd like to get one more promotion before I get out. We could use the money."

"We'll be fine," Ruth said, stopping short of mentioning a return to teaching at Ruhl School in Kansas City. George never spoke of it.

"If we start a family the extra money would be nice," George said. He studied her face in the afternoon light. "Besides…I'm not sure this is the time to get out of the service. All those guys who were in such a hurry to get out of the Army are still looking for jobs. I've talked to some of them."

"How about going back to the University," Ruth said. "Get a Master's degree."

"I'd like to," he said. "But after that…I'm not so sure I want to go back to teaching elementary school."

In her letters to her family Ruth had told them she and George would be back in Kansas City in September when George's tour of duty ended, ready to start the fall term at what was now named Ruhl-Hartman School.

He shrugged. "I like teaching, but not elementary school. And going back to Kansas City, it just won't seem the same as it did before the war."

"What do you want?"

"I want to see more of the world."

Michael George Trial
September 14, 1946

Mr. and Mrs. George T. Trial

"We talked about a family."

He put his arms around her and pulled her close. "I want that too."

"Well I have news for you," Ruth said shyly. "I'm pregnant."

A smile grew on George's face until he was beaming.

Ruth returned to Kansas City to be near her family when the baby was born. In the second week of September, 1946, George rode the train to Kansas City for the birth of their son Michael on September 14, 1946, at Menorah Hospital.

While he was this close, George rode the train north to Atchison to visit his mother. She was waiting for him at the train station. She beamed as she saw him and they greeted each other as they always had, not hugging. From the station he drove her Studebaker down the familiar gravel roads while they spoke of minor things—the weather, the crops, and the five Guernsey cows she kept.

"Pastures are so dried up I may have to feed some hay, and winter's not even started," she told George. "Could you pitch down some hay while you're here, Talbert?"

The image of the old barn back at the farm outside Muscotah came to his mind. He remembered standing in the shade in the loft and looking at the flat prairie undulating in the summer heat. In the bitter cold in the bombers over Germany he used to dream of those fields in the white sunlight and the thin prairie wind.

"Turn here, Talbert. You're about to the miss the turn."

George kept going. "Thought I'd drive through Muscotah on our way to Effingham. Just see what it looks like these days."

"Town's shrinking," Grace said. "People are moving to Atchison where the jobs are. Farms are consolidating. Most of the land's owned by big agriculture companies. They hire men to drive to and from Atchison every day to farm. High school's closed, not enough kids."

He drove down tree-shaded Third Street to the high school. The brick building looked much the same, but the grass around it wasn't cut.

"A shame, isn't it," Grace said, "that building sitting empty."

118

He turned around and drove by it one more time, thinking of the hot summer night he had graduated. Muscotah had been his whole world then; now it just seemed like the end of the world, peopled mostly by ghosts. They drove past the church, abandoned and falling into ruin. George remembered Reverend Beasley's words long ago, "God never abandons us."

He stopped the car and stared at the sagging building. "Maybe he does sometimes," George thought to himself. He remembered all the effort that Beasley had put into raising money to have that church built, how proud he had been when it was new, and how quickly he had left Muscotah when he had been offered a better position at a church in Topeka.

George silently thanked his mother for showing him that spirituality did not reside in that building.

Grace said nothing as George drove down the long road to the cemetery at the edge of town. They stood in the shade of a big elm tree looking at the headstones. The only sound was the rustle of the leaves in the breeze. A bit of shadow from an elm tree lay across his father's grave and George thought that very appropriate. There was always a bit of darkness behind his father's smile. The two of them stood for a moment; George felt the familiar prairie wind at his back, the heat of the sun in a cloudless sky.

Then they drove to Grace's tiny house on her twenty acres at the edge of Effingham. While she prepared dinner, he looked through the scrapbooks she had made of the war years—pictures cut out of Life magazine, a map that showed the American bases in England. Then they sat down to a big dinner of chicken and green beans and mashed potatoes.

He slept on the couch. This house had electricity, and George had made arrangements to pay for an electric water pump so Grace would no longer have to carry water from the hand pump at the cistern.

Next morning at breakfast, he found she had a new tablecloth on the table—a crude pattern of white sailboats on a picturesque ocean. He smiled thinking his mother would choose this pattern. She'd never travelled farther than three hundred miles from this farm in her whole life.

"Ruth and I want you to come to Washington next September for Michael's first birthday," George told her. "I'll send you the train ticket."

She smiled. "I'd like that."

After breakfast George helped his mother do some weeding in the garden, then wandered down to the old barn. It was dusty, with the pervasive but not-unpleasant cattle smell. He climbed the ladder to the hayloft, swung open the loft door, and stood staring out at the farmland.

Before he left, George took his mother's picture standing in front of her house. Later back in Washington when the photos had been developed, he sat at his desk staring at the photo and thought with a certain admiration, "My mother has lived modestly her whole life, never complaining, accepting the work, the loss of her husband, and that her only son wants to live elsewhere. She has accepted all this without bitterness or complaint."

Soon Ruth brought baby Michael to Washington, D.C. They rented a bigger apartment in a brick building in Georgetown, within sight of the Key Bridge, and settled into their new life. In the years to come, Ruth would think of these two years as some of the happiest times of her life. She realized one day, as she was quietly dusting the couch while the baby napped, that she had not sat daydreaming for months. Maybe when you have all you've ever dreamed of, you don't dream any more.

In September of 1947, Michael turned one year old. George and his mother and Ruth held a small celebration in their apartment and stepped outside to take some pictures. The four of them toured the monuments and sights of Washington. It was the first time his mother had ever been to a city except Kansas City, and George enjoyed showing her around. When her train had pulled out of Union Station, George and Ruth and Michael strolled out to catch the bus back to Georgetown.

"You look a little unhappy," Ruth said. "Sad to see your mother go?"

"No, I'm just not looking forward to going back to the office tomorrow morning. But I'm happy to have a job. All those other guys who were in such a rush to get out of the Army are now unemployed, living hand to mouth. But I'll admit I'm bored with my job. I just wish I had some kind of interesting assignment coming up, something I could really get my teeth into."

Ruth smiled again. "Want to write another book?"

"Maybe, but I need something to write about..."

"Distant horizons calling again, are they?" She was still smiling, but an edge of concern had crept into her smile.

"Don't you worry. Wherever we travel, we'll travel together."

"Promise?"

"Promise."

Monday morning George was in his office staring gloomily at the top of his gray steel Army issue desk. He felt his mind creaking under the deadening boredom and bureaucracy of the peacetime military.

There was a knock on his office door and Lieutenant Colonel Harry Snyder stuck his head in.

"Daydreaming?"

"No, planning."

Snyder took a typed form out and showed it to George.

"Congratulations!" George said, rising to his feet and throwing Harry Snyder a snappy salute. "Colonel Snyder."

"With a new assignment," Snyder said. He sat down and started talking.

In the summer of 1945, the U.S. Army had hurriedly constructed a string of temporary airfields across the Middle East to ferry the bombers of the Eighth Air Force across Asia to the Pacific theater.

When Japan surrendered, these bases were quickly abandoned. But now, with escalating Middle East tensions and the beginning of the Cold War, the need for the U.S. to protect Saudi Arabian oil fields had become apparent.

Harry Snyder had been assigned to renovate the airfield at Dhahran, Saudi Arabia. He rolled a map out on the gray steel desk and pointed to the Persian Gulf. "Right here." There was a lot of empty white space on the map around that point where the desert met the Persian Gulf.

"Standard Oil's had a camp there since 1936. They've built wells and a small refinery with offshore piping so tankers can load oil. And right now, the only protection it's got is from the British over on Bahrain Island about twenty miles away."

Saudi Arabia
Location of Principal Tribes Shown in Red

George and Harry sat down and put their feet up on their desks. "My assignment will be to get the airfield repaired," Snyder continued. "I'll be stationed here in Dhahran. My job will be to get it back into working order. Get some maintenance facilities built for B-17s and C-47s, shop facilities, a hangar, fuel dump, some temporary housing for a small detachment, maybe thirty men. I figure about a year…"

George grinned. "More likely two years, out there in the middle of nowhere."

Snyder shrugged. "Maybe."

"You looking for recruits?" George laughed, picking up the list of men to be demobed.

"Maybe. You interested?"

"Maybe. Beats this."

"There's one other thing. The State Department agreement with the Saudi government requires us to train the local Arabs as part of our mission. Basic mechanic and construction skills."

George watched the trees outside his window. It looked like it might be raining by the time he got back to the apartment tonight. "Any accompanied tours?"

"My wife Olive will come out to join me after six months, once I get the living quarters up to snuff. After that, if everything is coming along, I expect to get authorization to build ten units of married quarters."

"I'll go," George said. They shook hands.

The next day George sat at his desk fiddling with a pencil. "Ruth is expecting the three of us to go back to Kansas City, get back into teaching," he said to himself. He straightened the papers on his desk and stepped to the window. Fall had come to Washington; leaves from the big oak trees lining L Street were swirling into little piles along the sidewalks. He stood at the window watching the leaves whirling. He raised his eyes to the stone buildings across the street. I'm thirty-seven years old, he thought. I've been to Iceland and England. Do I want to stop now, go back to Kansas City, live the rest of my life there?

Harry leaned in the door. "Better get those maps prepped for the briefing at 1300."

George went back to his desk and back to work. But for the rest of the day his mind was elsewhere. He was in the hayfield back at his mother's farm, it was a summer afternoon, he had been in the loft pitching hay and had stood at the open door looking as far as he could see. The whole world was on the other side of that horizon.

That evening in the apartment after dinner, George sat smoking his pipe and watching baby Michael play with wooden blocks on the carpet. He was a quiet, happy child, content to play with whatever toys were at hand.

"Anything on your mind?" Ruth called from the kitchen where she was washing dishes. "You've been rather silent the last couple of days."

"Thinking," he called.

She stepped into the room.

"Harry Snyder offered me an assignment overseas. I want to take it. It's only for a year."

"What about me and Michael?"

"You'll join me as soon as we get housing built."

"What do I do while you're gone? Raise Michael by myself in this one bedroom apartment?"

George strained to think of the right words; the conversation was not going the way he had envisioned it. "You could move back to Kansas City. Your mother keeps saying she wants you to come for a long visit while Michael is still a baby. Let her help you. That's what she wants."

"But it's not what I want," Ruth said.

George watched the cars on the Key Bridge. It was strange to see so much traffic, the bridge lights on, car headlights, no blackout. "We'll be together within a few months."

He didn't notice the strange look Ruth threw his way. "So we'd be living in base housing, just like at Fort Leavenworth?"

George turned his back on the window. "Similar, yes. Was that so bad?"

"No," she said after a moment.

George sat down beside her on the couch. Michael had dozed off and they laid him on the couch with a blanket over him.

"I liked our place at Fort Leavenworth," Ruth said, looking fondly at Michael.

George breathed a silent sigh of relief.

"Where is this assignment?"

"Saudi Arabia," he said with great trepidation. Ruth said nothing.

Chapter 8

On Saturday morning, March 6, 1948, the C-47 carrying George and eight other Air Force men landed at Dhahran Air Base.

The sun had come up as they were flying south over the desert and George had gotten a glimpse of endless sand, aquamarine Gulf water, and a small airfield as the plane banked for a landing.

After a few minutes the door opened, and George gathered up his B4 bag and stepped out into a windy, cloudy morning dense with humidity.

"Major Trial?" someone said.

George turned and saluted the American colonel approaching. "Yes, sir."

"Welcome, George." It was Colonel Snyder, George's boss from the Washington, D.C. days.

He slapped George on the shoulder and they shook hands. "Welcome to Dhahran Air Base. We're pretty informal about military protocol here."

An Arab driver drove George in a Jeep to his quarters, a recently erected U.S. Army Quonset hut, one of a row of six identical huts. On the long flight to Saudi Arabia George had decided to start a journal, and he noted his arrival time and the weather in a terse note in a spiral notebook.

As he was unpacking, there was a knock on the door and Major Harry Sessums stuck his head in. "Welcome to Saudi Arabia," he said. They shook hands.

It was good to see his office-mates from the Washington, D.C. days. "I'll show you around," Sessums said.

They spent the rest of the day touring the classrooms, offices, and industrial facilities of the base.

The first group of Saudi students was assembled outside and George was introduced to them as a group. They were studying a curriculum that included basic and technical English. After their training, the students would be assigned by the Royal Saudi Air Force to operate Dhahran Air Base.

Late in the afternoon George was introduced to Major Salim, the senior Saudi military official on site. He greeted George warmly. "Please tell me if you need anything," he said in excellent English.

George later learned that Major Salim had been educated in London, which was not uncommon for sons of wealthy Saudis.

That evening, after a steak dinner at the tiny mess hall, George collapsed into his bunk. The next morning Colonel Snyder briefed him on his duties, the objectives of the training mission, and the assignments of the Americans on site. George also met several of the Egyptian instructors who had been hired to help teach and translate since they were fluent in Arabic and English.

George began teaching immediately, and the days flew by. Less than two weeks later, one of the Saudi students complained of severe stomach pain. George conferred with Colonel Snyder. There were no medical facilities on the base, so an American B-17 was ordered down from the U.S. base near Athens. George accompanied the student on the twenty-minute flight to Bahrain Island, where he was admitted to the British hospital and operated on for appendicitis.

George found the Saudi students bright and enthusiastic, but the Egyptian instructors were 'prima donnas,' considering themselves far superior to the Saudi bedouins. The students were very friendly and surprisingly well-informed on international issues. They were especially outraged by American support of the partitioning of

Palestine to form an Israeli state, and asked George endlessly why the American government would do such a thing. George found he had no answer for them.

Major Salim indicated that more students were coming and asked the U.S. Air Force to construct more housing for them.

Colonel Snyder and George talked with the American foreman for Bechtel International, who had a large workforce doing a variety of construction projects for the oil company ARAMCO, but the company was fully occupied and the request could not be accommodated.

On March 23, the local governor of the region—a Saudi prince—came for a visit to the area and George attended his first traditional Saudi gathering. A hundred people sat cross-legged on Persian carpets laid on the sand floor of a huge tent. A whole roast sheep was placed in front

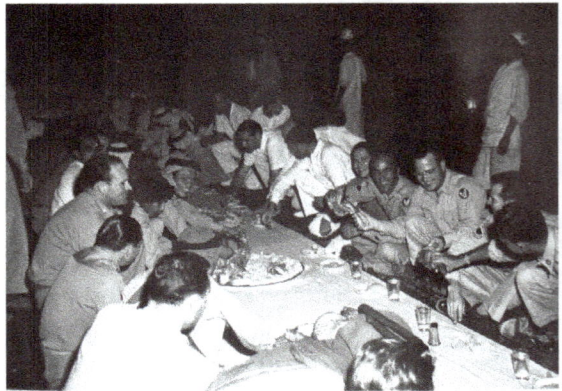

of every four people, along with plates of sweet bread, flat bread, rice, tomatoes, oranges, chicken, and apples. It was a huge feast.

Afterward, as the Americans left, George had a glimpse of the Prince conducting an audience in which any one of his subjects could speak directly to him, to pledge his family's allegiance or to make requests. "Called a *majlis*," Harry Sessums told George as they drove back to their quarters. "Just as it's been done since biblical days."

The next day, George's trip to the oil terminal at Ras Tanura was cancelled because of a dust storm, which the Saudis called a *shamal*. Visibility dropped to twenty-five feet and everyone had to breathe through cloth filters because of the sand and dust in the air.

George's planned curriculum, which Colonel Snyder approved, was to have the Saudi students learn 1,600 basic English words and 1,000 technical English words. Colonel Snyder cautioned the American officers about discussing religion with the Saudis, and under no circumstances were the Americans to try to convert Saudis to Christianity. This was not a problem for George since, for him, religion had always been a personal matter.

George was sometimes lonely, usually in the evenings, when the slow desert sunset turned the sky orange and silkened the cooling air. He often walked around the air base, just for the exercise. It cleared his mind. He missed Ruth and Michael, he wanted the family to be together, but he also enjoyed being alone. It was a feeling he never tried to communicate to others, not even Ruth, because it seemed so different from what others said they felt.

There was a small Christian fellowship group among the Americans and George sometimes attended, mostly because he knew that in a tiny community like this one, one needed to fit in, and because there was little else to do in the evenings. He listened to readings from the bible and joined in the discussion, but he knew there was deeper spirituality in the desert dawns he saw each morning than there would ever be in any book or sermon. His mind was often on Ruth and the baby. Out of curiosity one night in his quarters he read the Book of Ruth in the bible, looking for clues as to why Mack and Juna would have named their youngest daughter Ruth.

"Ruth is helpful and loyal," George whispered to himself. He closed the book and sat daydreaming at his desk, lulled by the ubiquitous air conditioner. He liked thinking about history and he liked being this close to where civilization had existed for

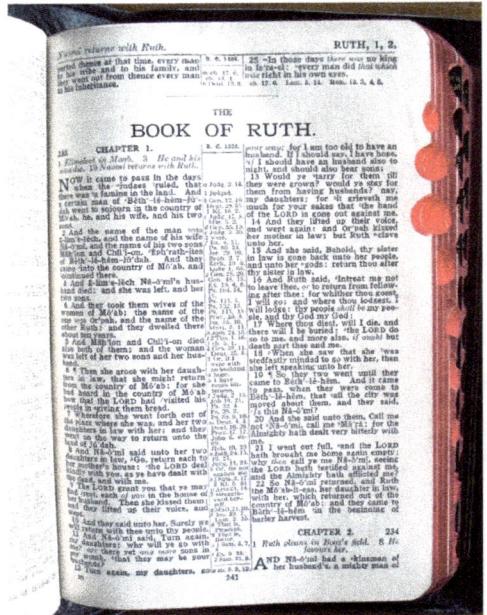

thousands of years. He had brought Everyman's Library copies of Herodotus and Thucydides with him, and had found a history book that contained descriptions of Ur of the Chaldees, Babylon, Palmyra, Queen Zenobia, Aleppo, and the Crusader castles. "What ridiculous slaughter, death by wound and disease. Trying to capture Jerusalem..." George muttered to himself as he read.

Throughout his life he attended church regularly, but he also kept his thoughts on religion and God and spirituality to himself. He found the bible interesting, but most of the preachers he'd known back in the States were not thoughtful people. George's mother had shown him by example that it is better not to discuss your religious views with others.

The Americans' only construction manpower on the base was a ragtag group of thirty Italian soldiers. 'Prisoners of war' left over from Mussolini's abandoned army in Ethiopia, they were still waiting for transport back to Italy. They were a cheerful lot, most of them skilled carpenters and pipe fitters, and they were making good progress in constructing the base facilities.

Most evenings after George had finished working on his assignment, his thoughts would drift to Ruth and baby Michael. ARAMCO had arranged for TWA flights to stop at Dhahran Air Base weekly, since they carried mail that reached the States faster than the military mail service. George had fallen into the expectation of getting a letter from Ruth every Thursday, and he was quite disappointed on the rare weeks when he did not.

On April 25, Colonel Snyder broke the bad news to the men that family housing would not be available until next fall at the earliest. George reluctantly wrote to Ruth with the bad news and hoped for the best.

In Kansas City, Ruth was lonely. Living with her parents in their small house was irritating for everyone. She felt restless and unhappy. She looked forward to George's regular letters, but he never was able to set a date when she could join him in Dhahran. She often wished they were together again, back at the apartment in Georgetown. That had been perfect.

She still read or daydreamed after lunch each day while Michael napped, and didn't hesitate to use her imagination to make up stories of faraway places to tell baby Michael, most of them embellishments of the stories she had told herself as a girl. There was a late-season snowstorm in March and Michael enjoyed being pulled in his sled through the snow.

Ruth sometimes told Michael about the big back yard of her childhood house in the village of Sandstone, Missouri. She recalled how the grass smelled in summer sunshine and the soft sound of oak leaves rustling on the big trees. She put these thoughts in her letters to George.

When he read of her unhappiness with living at her parents' house, waiting endlessly for housing in Dhahran, George was disconcerted. He wrote back immediately that he was doing all he could to get Colonel Snyder to authorize family housing. But her obvious unhappiness worried him.

Early in May he rode the military flight to Beirut, Lebanon. He met with several of the faculty members of the American University of Beirut with the intent of having the Saudi students attend a summer course there. AUB was a well-respected University on a beautiful campus overlooking the city and the Mediterranean. George dreamed of getting his Ph.D. and being a professor of history at a university like this one.

The city of Beirut was beautiful. A cosmopolitan city with tree-shaded boulevards, it had a residual sense of the French colony it had once been. Mountains rose behind it and the blue Mediterranean lay before it. Recently there had been demonstrations in the streets over American support of the British plan to establish an Israeli state by force, right in the middle of Palestine. George was grieved by the obvious wrongness of a foreign policy his country would pursue out of ignorance, a policy which would cause decades of suffering in the Middle East.

In Kansas City, Bonnie had made it clear to Ruth that she preferred to be alone when she came home from her teaching job. Ruth helped Juna around the house, but resented being treated as a child and as an unpaid housekeeper by her mother. She worried about her father. Mack was retreating into himself more and more each day. He had become a stick figure of a man, sitting alone by himself, or watching Michael play.

Mack sometimes confused his boyhood farm with the farm where they'd lived in Sandstone. Those years in Nevada had been good ones—on the farm at Sandstone and later in the house at 305 Central Avenue. Ruth remembered her father when he was young and strong and the future seemed as bright as a newly minted dime. His friends and neighbors would greet him as he drove down the street or stopped in the café for a cup of coffee. Mack liked people, so buying and selling real estate had been easy. He was an honest man and clients trusted and respected him.

As Ruth watched her father holding Michael, she sometimes wondered what things would have been like if they had not moved to Kansas City. Ruth hadn't wanted to move. She had loved Nevada; the town square, their house on Central Avenue, how proud she had been when her big sister Bonnie had let her walk with her the six blocks to Cottey College. She remembered the day the whole family had been in the audience when Bonnie had graduated. And she also remembered how sad she had been when Bonnie had left

for Kansas City. But Bonnie was bright and ambitious, eager to make her own way. Ruth remembered hiding in her room when Bonnie and her mother had gotten into terrible arguments over Bonnie moving away. But Bonnie was hard-headed and in the end she had got her way. They'd seen her off at the train station one hot July day. She had her new leather suitcase and was well-dressed in a striped dress, a hat, and white gloves. On her way to Kansas City where she had a teaching job waiting for her.

Her father was dozing, so Ruth gently disengaged Michael from his arms. She stood for a moment looking at her father and listening to the doves and the mournful sound of a faraway crow. She knew his mind was becoming cloudy. He would sometimes think he was at the farmhouse in Sandstone, hearing the meadowlarks out in the fields at evening. He'd say he needed to go help his father cut and rake the hay. Juna cared for him as he declined, lovingly and conscientiously, but with a bit of distance that troubled Ruth. She knew that distance was caused by her father's refusal to go with Juna to her many church functions. Ruth never argued with her mother, but she felt the same way her father did—religion was something between you and God. You didn't need to talk about it, you didn't need to go to a special building to pray, none of that was important.

Ruth put Michael down for his nap, then went back out to sit by her father in the sun on the back porch. He had left Nevada thinking he could sell real estate in Kansas City, but the stock market crash and the depression had come and they had lived on Bonnie's salary instead. The years had gone by and now he was a frail old man.

Ruth drifted back into the house and stood vacantly in the living room staring at the books on the shelves. Juna came in to get her bible off its shelf. "Read with me," she said in a tone just short of imperious. Ruth dutifully got her bible and sat on the sofa while Juna began reading in a low voice from the book of Isaiah.

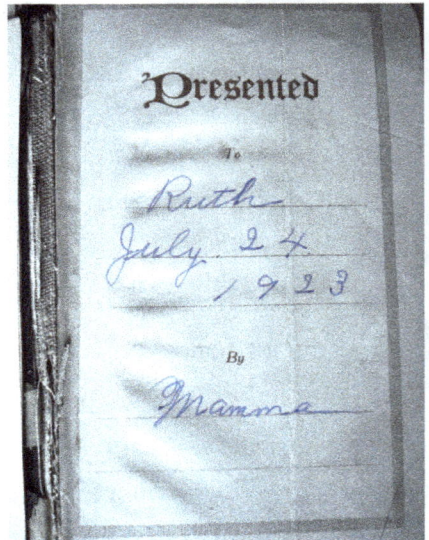

Ruth opened her bible to the front, where the inscription read, To Ruth from Momma July 24, 1923—her eleventh birthday. She remembered that birthday very well. They had eaten cake and homemade vanilla ice cream under the big elm tree in the back yard of the house on Central Avenue. She had gotten a doll and new shoes and a new dress, and this bible. In Nevada Ruth had enjoyed church-going—the social ritual, seeing friends, singing.

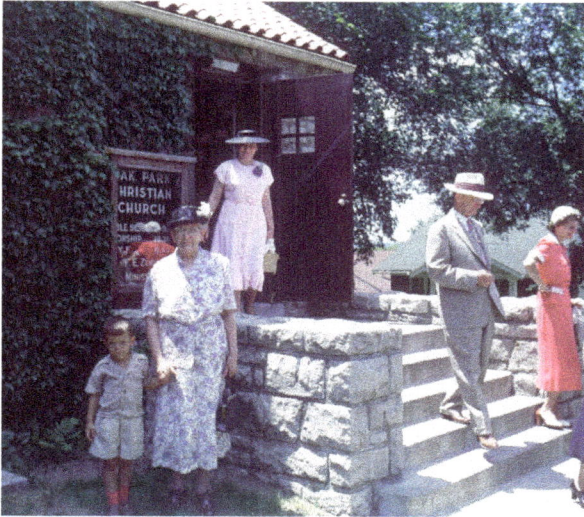

Little of the bible's lessons had made much impression on her, but she had a deep sense of reverence for all of nature.

Ruth and Michael went with Juna to church Sunday mornings, but that was all Ruth could stand of the dour moralizing Juna's friends liked to engage in. All Juna's friends were from the church. She taught one bible class and attended another one. She hosted the ladies in her

own home once a week and met at their houses twice more each week, none of which improved Juna's disposition. Only when Ruth's brother Jack visited was Juna her old self, cheerful and considerate.

"Now you read some to me," Juna said.

Ruth flipped to a passage at random and read until she heard her mother begin to snore softly, then she set her bible aside and made her way quietly down the stairs to the basement. The chair by the furnace was empty. Ruth found Bonnie standing on the walkway beside the house. She had her coat off even though it was cold in the shade. A cigarette butt had been stepped out on the concrete at her feet.

"Had enough of God for a while?" Bonnie said sarcastically.

Ruth felt her temper flare up. "I've had enough of all this!" she snapped, then clapped her hand over her mouth, shocked by her own outburst.

"You don't have it so bad," Bonnie said slowly. "You have George, and while you're here you can spend your time taking care of Michael. They leave you alone. I'm the one they expect to take care of the roof leak and the torn screens, the electricity bill, and oh by the way, pick up some milk at the market on your way home."

"I'm sorry," Ruth said. She looked down at the cracked concrete. "I know my being here is a burden too, even with the money George sends. But we'll be gone soon. I want to get settled in my own place. Even if it is just military housing, it'll be better than this place." She realized immediately that it was the wrong thing to say—Bonnie was settled here, and this place would likely be the only place she would ever live.

Bonnie changed the subject. "Mother is drifting off into some strange religious world."

"She tries to be righteous and moral," Ruth said.

"Too righteous." Bonnie pulled out another Chesterfield, then pushed it back into the pack. "Mother has taken all the joy out of religion and just left the righteousness and intolerance." She brushed by Ruth and went into the house. Ruth stood for a moment, then went into the bedroom where Michael had wakened from his nap and was happily playing with his wooden blocks.

"Let's go outside." She dressed him in his snowsuit, got out the red sled George had made, and pulled him along through the snow.

As she pulled the sled through the glittering snow she spoke—at first just a murmur, then quietly out loud into the silent sparkling day. "Bonnie has given up her own life to take care of mother and dad. She has no beau, few friends, only responsibilities. And now it's too late for her to build her own life. She's too old to get married, have kids, have a home of her own. Michael and I will leave soon. Mother and dad will die. She will be alone."

Ruth stopped and looked at the brilliant snowy sidewalks and the quiet street, the bare limbs of the elm trees. She trudged along pulling the sled until her tears dried.

At home she began composing another letter to George with the inevitable question: when would they be together?

> Col. Snyder had another housing conference
> with the base commander.
> 20 May – Thursday – This is the day.
> Thinking of 1940 all day.
> Received your letter of may 14ᵗʰ. Surprised
> that you were on a trip to Astor.

May 20, 1948, was George and Ruth's eighth anniversary. He reread all Ruth's letters one by one, then closed his notebook and stepped outside into the desert evening. The air was motionless, the sun a red globe prepared to set in the western sky. The stone wall behind him was still warm from the afternoon sun. For a moment George was back on his mother's farm in Kansas standing at the door of the hayloft, looking out at the heat rising off the scrubby alfalfa field. The two horizons became one in his mind's eye. The orange sphere of the desert sun flattened and sank in silence.

"If only Ruth and Michael were here with me," he whispered.

Chapter 9

In the days just before Christmas 1948, the Wallace household was bustling and happy. Ruth, Bonnie, and Michael, now two years old, were going to meet George in Rome for a five day vacation. Two days on the train, overnight at a hotel in New York, then thirty hours on a TWA DC-6 with four stops for refueling, and they were there, exhausted and excited.

George was waiting at the gate at Fiumicino Airport as they came up the steps on wobbly legs. He hugged Ruth and picked her up off her feet while baby Michael watched, puzzled. Then he kissed Bonnie on the cheek, which was very unlike him. They

made their way through immigration and customs, and walked out into the pale winter light. In the distance Ruth saw rows of Tuscan pines along the far hills, just like in the illustrations of Imperial Rome in her bible. It was clear and cold and windy—Ruth felt wonderful. There was still the occasional pile of rubble along the way to their hotel from the war just five years ago, but there were also lots of Fiats on the roads, and the people looked busy and prosperous. At the Savoy Hotel George had booked two large rooms, each with a private bath and a balcony that overlooked the boulevard below.

After unpacking they set out to explore, looking at the shops and restaurants and stretching their legs after the long flight. After a while, George hired an open carriage and they rode to the Borghese Palace.

Bonnie took Michael for a short walk while Ruth and George stood, arms around each other.

"Bonnie seems different," George said to Ruth.

"In what way?"

He shrugged. "Not her usual outgoing self. Probably tired from the trip."

Ruth watched her older sister pointing out the sights to Michael. "Well, she will have been teaching at Westwood for twenty years next June. And taking care of mother and father for twenty years." George heard the guilt in his wife's voice and held her closer. She squeezed George's arm. "I'm really glad we invited her to come along on this trip."

George had the carriage give them a tour of the nearby sights—the Forum, the Arch of Constantine, and the Coliseum. George was in his element, chattering on and on about the Roman Empire and the Republic.

"This is where Marc Antony gave his famous speech in 44 BC—'friends, Romans, countrymen, lend me your ears...'"

Bonnie joked, "I could use some new ears. Mine are frozen off." The wind was cold.

"We'll go back soon," George said. "But let me get a picture of you three in the carriage."

While he was taking the picture, Bonnie confided in her sister, "I'm ready to go back to the hotel and get a nice cup of hot tea."

Ruth shrugged and whispered, "He loves history, loves to lecture, loves to travel."

At the hotel they had tea and cakes sent up to the room. It was already past five in the afternoon and Michael was asleep, so they decided to stay in for the evening. Bonnie discreetly withdrew to her room.

The next day was Christmas and they were prepared—with a makeshift tree the hotel provided and the gifts they had brought with them. The hotel sent up a lavish breakfast including poached eggs in china egg holders and a tea pot under a tea cozy. Michael was as interested in a flashlight he found in the dresser drawer as he was in his toys.

In the afternoon they visited the Trevi Fountain, turned off for the day. Then they went to the great marble

147

edifice of the Victor Emmanuel Monument. George bounded up the wide staircase to take pictures of the city from the top. Bonnie, Ruth, and Michael wandered at a leisurely pace.

Bonnie was very pensive. "I think I was happiest back at the farm in Sandstone, when we were kids," she confessed quietly. "Or maybe the first couple of years at the house on Central Avenue."

Ruth was shocked at this revelation. She tried to ignore the pang of dread she felt, hearing her big sister speak so wistfully of the past. Ruth could not think of a response.

"I spoke to someone who'd been down there recently," Bonnie continued. "The old house out at Sandstone is abandoned now, overrun with weeds."

Ruth racked her brain for a more cheerful topic. She wanted Bonnie to be the way she always thought of her, the one who she and Jack followed around, the brightest, the leader, sure of herself.

"I remember walking with you to Cottey when I was in high school and you were in college. We walked all the way down Third Street under the big elms."

Bonnie adjusted her scarf and turned to Ruth. "I'm glad you're happy, you and George. You'll have a good life together."

"I remember how proud Mother and Dad were the day you graduated. They had the photographer take picture after picture."

"Those pictures were horrible. The glasses I used to wear," Bonnie said ruefully.

"And I remember how sad we all were the day you caught the train for Kansas City to start your teaching job," Ruth added.

"I wasn't sad," Bonnie said. Ruth saw her put on her set smile. "I was eager to get to the big city. Nevada was too small for me. Now, I don't know..."

Pigeons wheeled around the marble statues. Ruth thought Bonnie was cheered up, but then she saw the smile slipping away again. "Jack was always Dad's favorite," Bonnie said, her tone fond and envious. But a real smile began to spread across her face again. "Remember how mother used to make us sit in the rocking chairs on the porch of the house on Central Avenue and read."

Ruth laughed. "You always managed to get away."

"You and Jack liked to read, I don't." Bonnie continued to stare at the great monument before them. "I wonder if Jack still reads those silly books about Mars and the jungles of Africa."

"I'm sure he does," Ruth said. "Doris buys them for him. She's really good for Jack. He found the right wife." As they stood in the wind, the city spread out around them distant and unreal, Ruth said softly, "But Jack wasn't Mother's favorite child, Bonnie, you were. Jack and I knew it and we didn't mind. We looked up to you then and we still do."

"Well don't," Bonnie said shortly.

Ruth kept her voice steady. "We always will, Bonnie. Also," her voice faltered, but she pushed ahead with what she wanted to say, "… last night George told me he wants to stay overseas. He says the promotion potential is good and the living conditions are improving. He wants me to join him."

Bonnie turned to look at her younger sister. "When will you go?"

"A few months from now, March maybe." Bonnie nodded. "I know it'll make it harder on you, taking care of mother and father and working too." George was making his way down the steps toward them.

Bonnie smiled at her sister. "I'll be fine. You go. You and George should be together."

Their flight back to New York left at noon the next day. They sat silently together in the echoing terminal.

"It's really been fun," George said to Bonnie. "We'll do more vacations like this once Ruth and I get settled into life at the air base."

Bonnie nodded. "Well," she said, "I hope it's reasonably comfortable out there. It sounds a little," she struggled to choose the right word, "primitive."

George, vastly relieved that Ruth had agreed to come to Dhahran, squeezed Ruth's hand. "It will be fine. No frills, but comfortable enough and it's perfectly safe. And from Dhahran we can make trips to the ancient cities of Iraq, Syria, Lebanon. See Babylon, and Ur and Palmyra, and…" Ruth and Bonnie's flight was announced. "Three more months," George said. He squeezed Ruth's hand. "Then we'll be together again."

After their plane had disappeared into the hazy sky, George walked slowly down the concourse, thinking. He could finish up his tour in Dhahran, leave the Air Force, and go back to teaching at Ruhl School. He and Ruth could buy a house out in the new housing developments in Prairie Village or Shawnee Mission and spend Sundays with Mack and Juna.

He stared at the row of Tuscan fir trees on the vista, and at that moment he knew he would never go back to teaching in Kansas City.

When Ruth and Bonnie got back to Kansas City, Ruth was reminded of the summer of 1935, when she had returned home after graduating from the University and found her parents were very different from the parents she remembered.

Now she saw them changed even more. Mack had become a ghost. Juna spent her

time entirely caught up in her church activities. She went to services three times a week, read the bible every day, and taught bible classes nearly every day.

Bonnie went to work, ran errands, or spent time sitting by herself in the old armchair by the furnace in the basement, smoking Chesterfields and reading in the wan light from the small basement window above her head.

Where had they all gone, Ruth wondered—the big sister she and Jack used to follow around the farm at Sandstone—Mack, the handsome, genial real estate man, pillar of the small Nevada community—Juna, who had read romantic novels like *Ships That Pass in the Night*.

The first day home, Ruth noticed the little bookshelf where the old books had been kept was now bare. "I stored them in the basement months ago," Bonnie said shortly. "They were just gathering dust. This place is hard enough to keep clean without all that clutter."

Ruth resolved that she and Michael would take Bonnie on excursions to the Nelson Art Gallery, or take the streetcar to the Plaza and eat ice cream at Wayand's, or take a blanket and picnic basket to Brush Creek Park.

Ruth began to sort her things—what she would take to Saudi Arabia, what she would leave behind. She put a photo of George in uniform in a box and wondered fleetingly why Bonnie's wartime flirtations had never come to anything. She felt the familiar guilt knotting her stomach. I should stay here and help Bonnie with the house and with our parents, she thought, but she also knew she would not. She mentioned it once to Bonnie. "No you should not," Bonnie had said in a flat voice that Ruth had never heard before. "You belong with George." The words hit Ruth like a slap. She felt her eyes tearing up. Bonnie turned and went out of the room.

It was mid-April before Ruth received her tickets and papers to go to Dhahran. She finished her packing the night before, then

tossed and turned until morning. The four of them and Michael ate a silent breakfast. Soon she heard the taxi honk his horn outside and it was time to go. In a daze Ruth gathered up Michael. The taxi driver came up the steps to the porch, tipped his hat politely, and took her two suitcases to the taxi. Her father was standing in the sun on the back porch, his favorite place these days.

"I'll say goodbye here," he said so softly she could barely hear him. She hugged him, then pulled away slowly as the tears came. Ruth kissed her mother's cheek, hugged Bonnie, and made her way down the steps to the taxi. The spring morning was pleasant and silent. From a tree came the mournful cry of a crow, a sound Ruth always associated with this pleasant part of Kansas City which had been her home for twenty years.

She got in the taxi and managed to wave to her mother and Bonnie. All the way up Paseo Boulevard she kept her face turned to the window so Michael would not see the tears.

At Union station, as she waited for her train on a hard wooden bench in the echoing main hall, she saw the handsome man her father had been, taking her along in the car down gravel roads in Vernon County, commenting on the farms they passed. "That's a good one," he would say, pointing out a neat farm. "Well kept, good soil and water." She remembered the easy confidence he exuded, leaning on a fence under the shade of an elm tree, talking farm talk with his neighbors. Once, just before they'd left Nevada, he said, "I liked the old farm at Sandstone." He smiled at his daughter sitting beside him. "But I was just not cut out to be a farmer." They rode in silence for a moment. "Sometimes I wish I had been."

In 1949, the trip from Kansas City, Missouri to Dhahran, Saudi Arabia took five full days. Ruth and Michael rode the train to New York, spent the night in a hotel, then boarded a DC-6 and flew thirty hours to Rome, with stops for refueling at Gander, Newfoundland and Shannon, Ireland. In Rome they spent the night in a hotel, and the next morning boarded a U.S. military air transport command C-47 for the long flight from Rome to Athens, where they refueled and loaded and unloaded cargo. A stop in Beirut to refuel, then over the Syrian Desert toward the Arabian Gulf. As the sun began to angle down into afternoon, Ruth watched the rows of dun-colored sand dunes go by, the tops burnt brown like rolls in the oven. There was absolutely no sign of human habitation.

Ruth was mesmerized by the stark beauty slowly rolling by below her. The afternoon light was slanting toward evening as the plane began its descent, circling over the aquamarine water of the Arabian Gulf. They flashed past an empty beach and Ruth caught a glimpse of an asphalt road stretching out toward the desert.

Then the plane touched down on the runway and they were rolling toward the tiny terminal building. When the plane came to a stop and the door was opened, Ruth gathered up Michael and her purse and stepped out into velvety evening air, desert air, indefinably scented and intriguing. She went down the four aluminum steps on legs weak from the long journey. She made her way toward the stone building with the Dhahran Air Base sign. Then she saw George in pressed khakis. They embraced, he picked up their son, and they made their way up the steps and into the small terminal building still radiating the day's heat.

"What time is it anyway?" Ruth asked, exhausted and disoriented.

"Six thirty p.m., April 24, 1949," George told her.

As they finished with immigration and customs, an American couple came up and George introduced Ruth to Colonel O'Keefe and his wife Rosalind, who smiled and said, "Call me Roz."

They rode in the back seat of a Jeep to a stone building that was their apartment. George said something to the Arab driver in Arabic, then carried Ruth's suitcases inside and stood tense and silent, waiting for her reaction to her new home.

Ruth was pleasantly surprised at how large and clean it was, still smelling of fresh paint. There was a living room/dining room, two bedrooms, a kitchen, and a bathroom. All the kitchen and bathroom fixtures were American, and the beds were made with what looked like new sheets and blankets and pillow cases. There were towels on the racks, and even a nice white tablecloth on the dining room table. There were plates, glasses, pots and pans in the kitchen. George opened the refrigerator door—there were a few essentials inside. "Once a week a cargo plane comes down from the military commissary at Rhein-Main, Germany," he explained. "But this evening, if you're not too tired, I'd like to go to the O'Keefe's for drinks and dinner. We won't stay late."

Ruth sank down in one of the chairs. "This is nice," she said. "Much better than I was expecting."

George went over and gave her a hug. "It's great to have you here, both of you. Things will be fine. There are a couple of other American families here already, a few kids for Mike to play with. There's nothing much to do, but we can fly for free on the military flights in and out of here. I want to take a trip up to Iraq, see the ruins of ancient Babylon. And to Beirut, which is beautiful, right on the Mediterranean. And to Jordan…"

Ruth chuckled. "Slow down, George, we just got here. Let's get

cleaned up, unpacked a little, and go to your boss's house for dinner."

The jeep came back for them at seven thirty and drove them to the O'Keefe's large stone house. Mike showed off for his father and burned off some energy climbing the wall around the backyard barbeque while Colonel O'Keefe grilled steaks and the four adults talked about life at the air base.

"If there's anything you need," Roz told Ruth, "please don't hesitate to ask me. I know it can seem a little intimidating at first, but it's actually quite comfortable here." Ruth was beginning to learn that overseas compound living was very similar to pioneer life on the prairie—everybody helped each other. "There's not much to do here…" Roz said.

"But we are building a movie theater." Colonel O'Keefe grinned.

"And we can visit al Khobar and Qatif, the local villages. And if you like the beach, there's plenty of sand," Roz laughed. Ruth liked Roz already.

"Hundreds of miles of sandy beach, absolutely uninhabited," George added. "Except for the little fishing and pearl diving village near the oases."

"There's pearl diving?"

"Before the oil company came to this area, pearl diving and fishing were the main occupations of the Arabs living here."

Roz caught her husband's eye. "We can take the Trials out on a dhow trip sometime. It's fun. We can hire a native sailboat—a dhow—to take us out for a day trip to Tarut Island. We'll take a picnic. Nothing on the island except some palm trees, but it's fun exploring. And we can drive down the coast road to where there used to be a town. Sometimes you can find ancient coins and bits of broken pottery."

Ruth's eyelids were drooping closed. Michael was nearly asleep in a chair, wedged in beside the younger O'Keefe boy. Roz smiled. "Sorry, I know you must be exhausted, and we're talking your ears off."

The same Jeep took them the two hundred yards to their apartment. Inside it was cool and fresh, smelling faintly of new paint and new furniture. Ruth got Michael to bed and took a quick bath. The bathtub was big and new and there was plenty of hot water, much better than their apartment in Washington or her parents' house in Kansas City. Wrapped in a new robe she found in the closet, she checked that Michael was sleeping soundly.

In the big new bed, George was snoring gently. Ruth slid under the sheets and lay in the darkness, completely relaxed. The big yard and the old elm trees at the house in Sandstone drifted across her mind and for a moment she felt a vague homesickness, not for

Missouri, but for childhood and all the times past.

As she drifted into sleep, she dreamed of the blue Arabian Gulf water and a sailboat under a full sail. What adventures lay ahead! But she also knew she was safe at home, with her husband and son.

Chapter 10

The nearest village to the air base was al Khobar. In 1949 it was a dusty collection of mud brick buildings without utilities of any kind, home to perhaps three hundred people who made their living by fishing and pearling in the Gulf. The main street had recently been paved, and since ARAMCO had begun selling gasoline from a makeshift gas station just outside the main gate, several cars, trucks, and home generators had been acquired. One of the primary trading concerns in al Khobar was the Green Flag

store, a general store run by a Lebanese man and his family.

On a glaringly hot Thursday afternoon, George checked out an Air Force Dodge Power Wagon and they drove the one kilometer to Khobar for some shopping. They arrived just as the store was reopening after midday prayer. After Ruth had made it clear to the Lebanese proprietor, who had retained some of his elementary school English, that she wanted Arab clothing for Mike, he and a son began bringing out armfuls of children's clothing in all shades and colors, all made in India. Eventually they chose a bright pink *thobe*.

"The head cover is called a *ghutra*," George explained as Mr. Khoury fitted a small headdress on Mike. "The red and white checked cloth is the color and pattern most Saudis wear, although on more formal occasions they wear white ones. The black cloth coils that hold it in place are called an *agal*. The gold braided agal is for royalty."

Eventually, after four changes of costume, it was done. They thanked Mr. Khoury profusely and returned home, where George took photos of Michael in front of their apartment.

"Your mother will be aghast when she sees these photos," George told Ruth.

"So will yours," Ruth laughed. Michael took it all in stride.

The heat was overwhelming against the rock wall of their apartment, so they went into the cool gloom of the interior.

"You know," Ruth said, "Michael really will grow up with a different perspective than kids his age back in Kansas City."

George nodded. "I don't think that's a bad thing."

The next morning, George, Ruth, and Michael had a leisurely brunch at the officers' club. All twenty of the American officers and their wives were there. Desultory conversations and table-hopping occurred as they did nearly every Friday.

After the brunch, Ruth and George walked Michael back down the street to their apartment. The day was already very hot. Ruth could tell George had something on his mind.

"How would you feel about going to India for a few days to do some sightseeing?" he said thoughtfully.

"How long a trip?"

"A couple of days, no more. I have two schools I'd like to visit—one in Bombay, one in New Delhi. The air attaché plane makes the trip twice weekly."

"I meant how long is the flight," Ruth said. "Michael was good on the flights coming over here, but I don't know about a really long…"

George smiled at Michael. "The old C-47s MATS uses for our

flights can go about a thousand miles at a hop, so five hours from here to Karachi, an hour on the ground to gas up the plane, then five more hours to Bombay."

Ruth took George's arm. "I'd love to see a little bit of India. When would we go?"

His expression became sheepish. "Day after tomorrow."

Ruth laughed. "For being such a good planner, you sure don't give me much warning. Fortunately your son and I have very few plans that can't be changed, do we Michael?"

Michael gave her a quizzical look, then dashed ahead and into their apartment.

"I guess someday we'll have to relearn to lock the house door. Fortunately that won't be until we go back to quote, civilization, unquote."

On the flight to India George spent much of his time in the navigator's seat talking to Captain Hays and Lieutenant Ryan. Ruth read A Handbook of India, which her new friend Dorothy Cretors had loaned her from their trip to India. Saudi Arabia censored all periodicals and books coming into the country, so there was very limited reading material at the informal lending library that Mildred Sessums had set up in a corner of the base administration office.

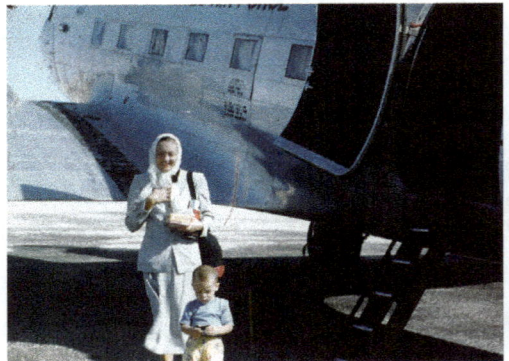

On the last leg of the trip, Ruth sat leaning against the aluminum window frame of the plane, staring down at the limitless blue of the Indian Ocean. Michael happily played with a worn toy truck, the one toy she'd allowed him to bring. They were the only passengers so he had the run of the plane. He made the aisle of the plane his own and he liked the netted compartment where embassy mail was stacked, but he wasn't allowed to climb the netting. He was an obedient boy who didn't have to be told twice and didn't whine.

Soon after the C-47 landed with a rattle and rumble on the cracked concrete runway, they taxied to the terminal and the door was let down. The plane's canned air washed away and the scents of India flowed into the plane. The air was humid and warm, but not oppressive. After the sandy glare of Arabia, everything seemed darker—the soil, the vegetation, even the sky.

They quickly passed through customs and got into an embassy car. "Nice getting the same treatment as the embassy people," George confided to Ruth as the car made its way into the city towards the Ambassador Hotel.

They had high tea in the dining room with four waiters hovering. The tea was the best she had ever tasted. "Makes me feel like somebody important," Ruth said self-consciously but happily.

"The last faint echo of British colonial days," George said. "British India was the centerpiece of Victoria's empire. No other colony had quite the effect on Britain that India did." They thanked the staff in the lobby and told the front desk they were going for a walk.

"Car and driver, sir?"

"No thank you, not today."

They turned off the main street and wandered down the back streets, the local kids staring at them as they passed. Michael was fascinated by a bullock cart.

"Michael, don't get too close," George warned. "But I do want to get a picture."

They walked on. The scents were not overwhelming, but incredibly varied. And behind them all was the sense of millions of people—not a dirty scent, not even unpleasant, but omnipresent.

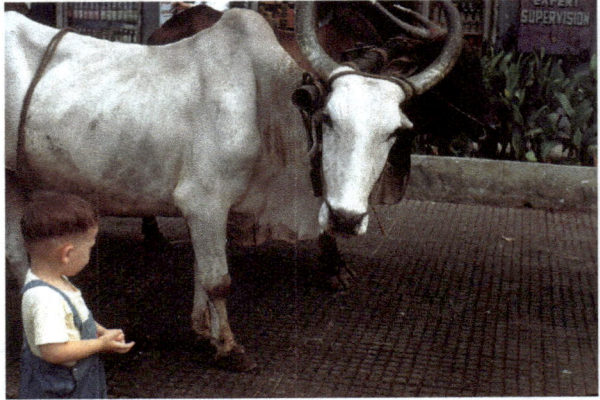

George caught a new scent and moved ahead like a hunting dog stalking a quail. Ruth and Michael caught up with him in front of a woodworking shop. Six men and two helpers were making furniture. "Sandalwood," George said.

"Welcome," the proprietor said, emerging from his office. All the workmen had stopped their tasks, passersby on the street stopped to stare, and soon the family was surrounded by a crowd all intent on what the foreigners were doing. The proprietor shouted the crowd away except for a handful of tenacious street urchins.

"These night stands are very nice," George told Ruth.

"Yes, very nice," the proprietor echoed.

Ruth looked at the matching night stands. "They are nice, but

I wonder if we should be buying furniture when we can use base furniture for free. And we don't know how long we'll be in that apartment either."

But George was captivated by the wood. One of the workmen opened the top and took all the drawers out for his examination. "Only fifty rupees," the proprietor said. "We will deliver to your hotel."

George and Ruth exchanged a glance, then George said, "Forty."

After a time they settled on forty-five.

With a great flourish, the workmen began wrapping the two night stands in filthy rags from the floor at the back of the shop. George watched Ruth's face run through a gamut of expressions.

George paid the man and told him to deliver the night stands to the Ambassador Hotel that night. "We are leaving tomorrow," he explained. Then the family made their way back to the hotel. As soon as the shop was out of sight, Ruth confiscated the piece of unidentifiable candy Michael had been given. They stopped by a Hindu temple while George got the obligatory photos. A crowd again gathered and they moved on.

"Do you really think we should have bought that furniture?" Ruth asked, frowning.

"Sure," George reassured her. "Captain Hays and I can secure it in the mail enclosure on the plane; it'll be fine. Oh, the dirty rags. We'll dispose of them at the hotel."

The next morning the embassy car picked them up at seven and took them to the military airfield where the battered C-47 waited. Ruth placed a sleepy Michael in their usual seats on the plane—four rows from the back, away from the engine noise and with a view of the ground from behind the trailing edge of the wing. George was settling in when Captain Hays leaned around from the pilot's seat and asked, "You want to take the left seat, sir?"

George grinned. "No, you fly, I want to sightsee. When we get to Agra make a swing around the Taj Mahal so I can get some photos."

Half an hour later Hays turned and waved at George, then put the plane into a long sweeping circle and there was the Taj Mahal below them, looking like some fantastic toy. George was at the window snapping photos. Ruth woke Michael and pointed out the window.

"That's it," she told him.

"What is it?" he asked.

"An Indian lady died a long time ago and her husband built this building to remember her. It's very famous and very beautiful."

On the ground they walked through rooms cool with white marble tile, listening to the soft echoes of voices from other chambers. They walked the length of the reflecting pool in hot Indian sunshine and George found someone to take their picture.

169

Back at the air base the following Friday morning, the family had their customary brunch at the officers' mess. Ruth stood to go when George caught her arm. "Not quite yet."

Luigi, the Italian chief cook, brought a cake to the breakfast table. Michael jumped back into his chair, grinning ear to ear.

"Not for you Michael, your birthday isn't for four more months. Happy anniversary Ruth," George said. "May 20, 1949. Married nine years." He gave her a hug and a kiss and they sat down to eat cake.

"So you had poor Luigi up at the crack of dawn making this cake?"

"Yes," George said proudly. "He loves doing this sort of thing. He's a natural born chef. He'll do well back in Italy."

"If he ever gets back," Ruth amended.

Two weeks went by and Ruth felt like she was fully settled into air base routine. George spent his days at the training center, working with the course schedule and teaching some classes himself. The first class of Saudi students graduated.

With that milestone, Ruth saw George truly able to relax at last. "You've really made progress," she told him and he smiled.

"So this weekend, to celebrate, let's explore," George said. Ruth laughed. "Always ready to travel aren't you?"

Friday, Islamic Sunday, was the usual white-hot glare as George drove the Air Force Dodge Powerwagon down the empty asphalt road twenty kilometers to the ancient oasis of Qatif.

The ruin of the fort sat abandoned and silent. "Let me get a photo of you and Michael," George said.

Ruth stuffed her handkerchief in the pocket of her skirt. "If my mother and Bonnie see this photo, they'll recognize this skirt. My old nurse aide skirt—still in service."

The building was roofless and sweltering hot. The three of them wandered through the rubble. "This was an outpost of the Ottoman Empire," George told Ruth. "The Empire lasted four hundred years, controlled trade all along the Arabian Gulf coast and the Mediterranean coast." All the wood from the roof and the doors had long ago been used for firewood by the local villagers.

"This place smells bad," Michael said.

"After the Turks were gone, Lawrence of Arabia tried to unite the Arab tribes," George continued, sweating, but loving to lecture. "But the British and the French, who'd just won World War One, didn't want a united Arab world. And the tribes didn't want that either." He clambered down from the top of the mud wall. "This place has probably been abandoned since World War One days."

"But I see it's still being put to use." Ruth pointed at a cluster of desiccated turds in a corner.

"Let's move on," George said. "The *suq* should be interesting."

It was much cooler in the *suq*, which was a row of open-fronted shops on a narrow street of mud brick buildings. They wandered past leather shops and brass shops and shops selling glass water jugs, tools, and harnesses for camels and donkeys. Each shop had a black sheep's wool awning. Ruth bought a brass coffee pot with a curved spout. "Every American has one of those," George said, but gave the vendor four *riyals* anyway.

They made their way back to the Dodge, where George gave ten *qursh* to the kid squatting in the shade 'guarding' their car. They started for home down the coast road. The tiny village was quickly lost from view in the expanse of white sand and aquamarine Gulf water.

"If oil production keeps increasing to meet demand," George said, "that whole village—the buildings, the camels, the donkeys, the old dhows, the tents, this whole way of life—will be gone in a generation. Oil money will sweep it away."

"That's a lot of change. Will their society weather the storm?" Ruth said absently. She slid Michael's sunglasses off his sleeping face and nudged him out of the sun.

"It will have to," George said. "The Saudis know they don't have a choice. The world needs oil. So they can either sell the oil and get rich, or have it taken from them by force once the world gets desperate."

"Today at ARAMCO I spent the afternoon with a guy named

Vince James," George told Ruth at dinner one evening, "which was a pleasant relief from talking to my staff."

Ruth served the roast beef and potatoes. She knew George had been growing increasingly unhappy the last few days. Maybe now he would talk about it.

"Your staff is all tech sergeants. Military guys are always going to grumble," Ruth said. "They are single guys out here for a year with no entertainment, no women. That's all it is."

George chewed stolidly for a moment, thinking this over. "That's true. All they talk about is doing their twelve months and getting back to the States. Even the three week trip to Beirut to take classes at the American University doesn't interest them. They make it sound like it's more of a burden that a treat."

Ruth knew how hard George had worked to arrange the training trip to AUB. "Well, they don't have the love of learning that we do."

"And they have no idea of how beautiful the AUB campus is, and the city of Beirut. Plus all the history in that area—the Roman city at Baalbek, the Phoenician cities of Sidon and Tyre…"

Ruth put her hand on George's arm. "We love history and exploring, but for them this is just another remote duty assignment. Not the Sessums or the Snyders, of course."

George finished eating and set down his utensils. "I really envy the ARAMCO guys like Vince James. The company has a broad education program, not just airfield operations, anything the Saudis want. They're not bound by the Air Force budgets. And they don't have to rely on a bunch of enlisted guys with no motivation. Everybody up at ARAMCO seems highly motivated."

Ruth cleared the plates and they sat together in the living room with a cup of coffee. Like many of the wives, Ruth had begun buying local coffee, locally roasted. She had also bought a hand-turn grinder. The fresh coffee was strong and delicious.

"Vince's wife dropped by his office while I was there, Lucy is her name. I told her you and Michael were here and they invited us to get together. They have two boys a little older than Michael."

Ruth sipped her coffee. "You don't seem so enthusiastic about it."

"They want us to go to the beach with them. Their boys love the beach. The water is warm, big sand dunes right down to the water."

"I know you don't care much for the beach, but we should go. It's a chance to make new friends and to let Michael play with somebody new."

George nodded slowly. "OK, I'll tell Vince we'd love to. He wants to go next Thursday afternoon, about three, after most of the heat of the day

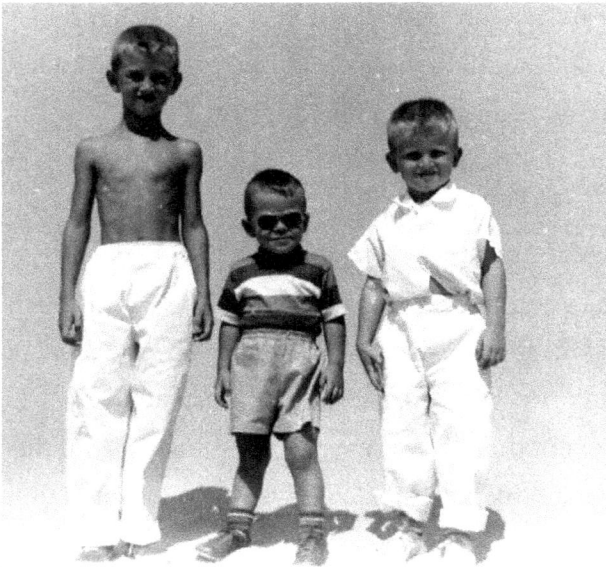

is past. We'll take barbecue stuff and have a picnic."

"Sounds wonderful."

And it was. The boys could slide down the sand dunes into the warm salt water. Michael loved paddling

around in the waveless shallows. Lucy and Vince James were very personable, unassuming, friendly people. They were both teachers who'd come to work for ARAMCO from Richmond, Virginia. Ruth was embarrassed by the makeshift suit she had made for Michael.

"Nonsense," Lucy reassured her. "No fashion statement here. And we all make our children's clothes, or pass them from family to family. Tommy," she pointed at her older son, "has on a swimming suit Linda Crampton gave me when her son

175

outgrew it. Jimmie will inherit it when it's too small for Tommy. It's frontier living here." She said it with pride, not embarrassment.

The hours flew by as they talked and laughed about their teaching days back in the States. As the sun neared the desert's edge the wind dropped away to nothing, the sky over the Gulf became mauve and lavender, and the air took on the unique silky feel of desert evening.

"This is absolutely gorgeous," Ruth said. The boys, tired from sun and play and salt water, had lain down on the reed mat Lucy

had brought. The adults fell silent. There was no sound whatsoever. The sky, the desert, the flat gulf waters were perfectly still. As far as the eye could see in all directions, the world was without any sign of other human beings.

Three weeks went by placidly. During a Wednesday night dinner at the officers' club, George and Major Ed Berringer got into a long discussion about military aircraft while Ruth sipped coffee and

Michael played under the table.

"The C-47 is one of the best planes ever built," George told Ed.

"Ten thousand of them built during the war," Ed added. "Two Pratt and Whitney R1830 twin row radial engines. Eighteen hundred horsepower each. Cruises at 10,000 feet, carries twenty passengers in civilian configuration."

"And it's a workhorse," George added. "Never breaks down and it's reliable, will fly into and out of very short runways…"

"But the toilet is a cold and drafty steel closet," Ruth laughed. "But at least there is one."

"Twelve hundred mile range," George continued unabashed. Ed drifted away.

George went to the dessert table and returned with three small slices of white cake with chocolate icing.

"I have a birthday treat planned for you," George told Ruth. Her birthday was the next day, July 24.

"Is this a treat for me or for you?" Ruth laughed. They ate their cake.

"All three of us," George confessed. They collected Michael and made their way out into the humid night for the short walk down the road to their apartment.

"We'll catch the Air Attaché flight up to Beirut," George continued. "I'll visit the American University there, then we'll drive to Jerusalem, Amman, and Damascus. And if we're not too tired, we'll continue to Aleppo and see the old crusader castle there." Ruth could see George was beaming—he loved history, and he loved seeing the bits of history in the countries all around them.

Ruth smiled and took his hand. "It's OK, it's dark. Nobody

177

will see us holding hands," she told him. "I hear you say Beirut is beautiful, and I'd love to see the Roman ruins in Lebanon and Jordan, and maybe a crusader castle or two. The crusades, King Richard the Lionheart versus Saladin."

"Great! I was hoping you would want to go," George said. "I wish I'd taken more history courses at the University in Columbia when we were there that summer, before I went on active duty. Remember how the campus looked that Spring?"

"Of course. I liked history and I liked Columbia too. Maybe someday we'll go back. You can get your doctorate, become herr professor." She knew he harbored a secret dream of getting his Ph.D.

The eves on their apartment building were dripping with condensation, but inside it was cool and dry and quiet. Ruth loved the warm light of the table lamps on their Persian carpet and the brass coffeepot and tray they'd bought. There was even a soft scent of sandalwood from the tables they'd bought in India.

They put Michael to bed and retired. George was asleep instantly, but Ruth lay awake—not restless, just perfectly calm, perfectly content, listening to the hum of the air conditioner. She slipped out of bed, went into the living room, and stood looking at the moonlight on the Persian carpet, the couch and chair, the tables, the brass tray and coffee pot. She thought about their trip to India, their visits to Khobar and Qatif, the picnic at the beach with the

James family.

She tried to envision how far she was from Kansas City, but it didn't seem real. After a while she realized how satisfied she felt. She was still living in Air Force base housing, but it felt different from back in the States, different from all the transfers their first year of marriage.

This felt like home.

Chapter 11

In Beirut, The Hotel St. George was right on the Mediterranean. They left the balcony doors open overnight and fell asleep listening to the gentle waves. As the sun came up over the Mediterranean a delightful breeze woke Ruth.

George was already up and dressed. Michael lay perfectly relaxed on the bed. Ruth smiled. "Good morning." George gave her a kiss. "We need to get up and going. Breakfast in the dining room then the car will pick us up to take us to the University."

Ruth shook her head. "These working vacations, you're always in a rush. The view is lovely and the air is so fresh and clean."

"Beirut is called the Paris of the Middle East," George stated, not listening. "But we need to get down to breakfast…"

"I know." She got up and began dressing. "Talk to the dean at the American University at Beirut this morning, then drive to Jerusalem, with a short visit to the Roman ruins at Baalbek on the way."

George packed while she dressed Michael. Then they ate a

wonderful breakfast on the terrace overlooking the Mediterranean before the car took them up the hill to AUB.

The American University at Beirut was on a hill overlooking the blue Mediterranean. "These stone buildings and red flowers are beautiful," George said. "And this ocean view is spectacular."

Mr. Ansara, the dean of the university, was waiting in his office

and they spent a pleasant fifteen minutes over delicious French coffee. "You'll find bits of French cultural influence here in Beirut, left over from colonial days," Mr. Ansara told them. He was a tall, cultured Lebanese man in a wool suit of French cut.

"I'll leave you two to talk," Ruth said when they'd finished their coffee. "Michael and I will stroll around the grounds."

The men stood. Mr. Ansara shook hands with her and smiled at

Michael. "A well-behaved boy you have here."

Ruth made her way out into the courtyard, chose a stone path at random, and strolled between azaleas and hibiscus. "You are a well-behaved boy, aren't you?"

"Look at that." Michael pointed at a fountain.

Students walked by, handsome young men and women, the women without veils, some wearing slacks. Ruth felt dowdy in her travelling skirt and blouse. "Descendents of the Phoenicians," Ruth told Michael as they walked. "Sailors and traders for three thousand years. They sold purple dye to the Romans for them to make their imperial togas."

A lawn sloped down to a low stone wall. The view of the Mediterranean was magnificent. Ruth sat on the wall savoring the cool air, the brilliant sunshine. "George will want to come back here," she knew. University campuses had a continuing attraction for him. "And I think I could live here, in Lebanon," she told Michael.

She thought of the campus at the University of Missouri and  her room at the boarding house her freshman year. How lonely she had felt after Bonnie had caught the train back to Kansas City. But after she had gotten to know some of her classmates and become familiar with the town and the campus, she had grown to love the University and the town. The classes were interesting, her roommates were fun. When she graduated, she had hated to leave Columbia. She remembered her tears as the train pulled away from Columbia.

She collected Michael and strolled down the curving walkway toward the rocky beach. "But that's the nature of University days— they end." At the concrete wall above the rocky beach the breeze was stronger.

That's the nature of overseas living too, she thought. Eventually

it ends. And when it ends, it ends completely. You can never go back.

"But I did go back to Columbia," she told Michael. "Your father and I." She remembered the vine covered house they rented and the neighbor's dog Mopsy. "It was the spring of 1946. He was completing his master's degree. I was pregnant with you. The war was over. We were very happy. Just like we are now."

She took Michael's hand and they started back up the walkway to the administration building. "You were almost born in Columbia, did you know that?"

"No," he said. "Where was I born?"

"In Kansas City, in Menorah hospital where I used to work."

George bustled out of the administration building right on cue, bubbling with enthusiasm. "Dr. Ansara sent for our car and driver. This is a wonderful institution. I am definitely going to do more summer sessions here for some of our Saudi students."

The three of them climbed into the battered Chevrolet and started off.

"Amman?" the driver asked.

"No," George said. "Jerusalem."

They drove up over the mountains behind Beirut and down into the desert.

"There are the Roman ruins." George pointed at a row of white columns. "The temple of Zeus at Heliopolis. This trade city used to be called Heliopolis."

Ruth laughed as they walked down the long colonnade. There was a hot wind from the desert blowing steadily toward the mountains.

"What's so funny?" George asked. "Let me get a photo."

"I remember my brother Jack reenacting his beloved Edgar Rice Burroughs books about Mars. One of the cities in those books was named Heliopolis."

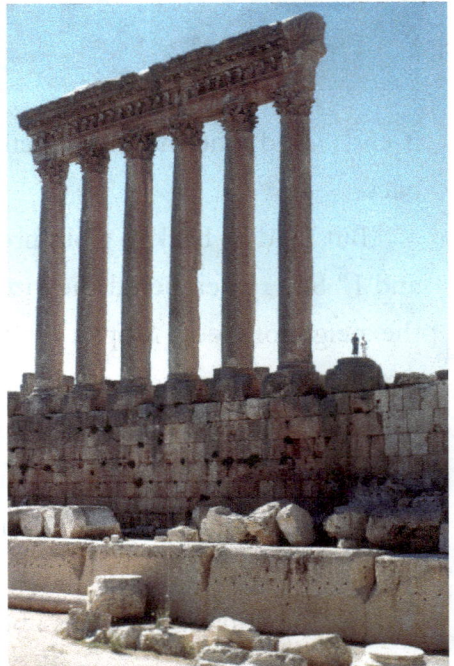

184

George glanced at the tourist brochure he'd brought and began his lecture. "This used to be a trade center on the caravan routes, close to the ports of Beirut and Tyre. The cedars of Lebanon were cut and the wood used for roof beams in temples and palaces from Egypt to Damascus to Baghdad to Rome itself."

They made their way back to the car. Their driver, a polite Lebanese man in a white and black checked ghutra, opened the back door for Ruth and Michael. George spoke to him in Arabic. "Yes, sir, now to Jerusalem," he answered in English.

An hour's drive across the desert brought them to the passport check at the Jordanian border. George chattered on and on about what a great university AUB was. Another hour of driving brought them to Jerusalem.

They toured the Dome of the Rock mosque, and Michael raced up to the pulpit. "Michael, the young Imam," George joked. Ruth motioned Michael down, "We don't want to be disrespectful," Ruth said.

They drove past the Wailing Wall to the Garden of Gethsemane and wandered among the dusty olive trees. The scent of sage and dust and history was in the air. They drove out to the

Kidron Valley and from a bare desert hill could see the Dead Sea in the distance. But by then it was late afternoon and George could tell Ruth and Michael were tired. He was a bit disappointed at their lack of interest. "It's a little less interesting than I was expecting," he said. "But I'm glad we've seen it."

Before they got back in the car he squatted down beside Michael and pointed, "that's the Mount of Olives from the bible, right over there. Those are olive trees." Michael dutifully looked in that direction. George had the driver take them back to town and they walked a little way up the Via Dolorosa.

"It feels much like the *suq* in Qatif," Ruth said to George.

"Same culture," he replied. "Parts of it unchanged for two thousand years."

That evening at the King David Hotel, they had a pleasant dinner of grapevine-wrapped chopped lamb and rice with spices. "Put lemon juice, like this." The waiter demonstrated. It was delicious.

"We've seen some of the Islamic and Christian and Jewish shrines here," Ruth said as they lay in their beds that night in the hotel room. "I guess it's not possible to see Mecca."

"Not unless you convert to Islam," George told her. "It's a closed

186

city to anyone who is not Moslem."

George had almost drifted off to sleep when Ruth spoke again softly. "Seeing Jerusalem and reading about religion, I'm struck by how similar Islam, Judaism, and Christianity are to each other. They all have a single god, a heaven and hell, an afterlife, a holy book, churches and priests."

"They all originated in this area," George said. "Centuries apart maybe, but culture didn't change much between the time Abraham was born down in Iraq, Jesus was born in Jordan, and Mohammed was born in Saudi Arabia. For many of the local people, life still hasn't changed much since the time those men were born and died."

"And yet so many lives have been lost over the centuries," Ruth continued in a soft but troubled tone. "So much suffering. Religions fighting each other."

George said nothing. Grace and Lloyd had taught him to keep religious opinions to himself.

They reached Amman late afternoon the next day. George got quite a kick out of the fact that locations were all in reference to which traffic circle was nearby. "Our hotel, the Philadelphia Hotel, is near circle two."

"Better to be in the inner circles than the outer circles." Ruth smiled.

"Lots of inner and outer circles back at the air base," George chortled. "Same as Fort Leavenworth before the war."

"Dorothy is so ambitious for her husband's career," Ruth said. "What is he doing stationed in Dhahran, out in the middle of

nowhere?"

George's grin faded. "Last year when I came, it was a good assignment. We were starting things up. Doing something really useful…but now it's settled into routine. I keep trying to expand the training program, but O'Keefe is not supportive. He wants to keep the training program low-key. He knows that if our program gets too visible, the State Department will give the Air Force brass a hard time about getting into State Department turf, and he wants to avoid that. He's on the promotion list for Brigadier General, no time to be rocking the boat."

The car pulled up in front of a hotel right across the street from a ruined Roman amphitheater. "On the other hand, ARAMCO is expanding their training program," George said as he got out.

The bellman collected their suitcases. George gave the driver twenty extra piasters. "Tomorrow at nine," he pointed at his watch.

"*Tisah.*" The man nodded and got back in his car and drove away.

"We'll explore tomorrow," Ruth told Michael.

That night in their big room, after they'd given Michael his bath and put him to bed, Ruth whispered, "Seems like ARAMCO gets away with doing what they want, regardless of what the State Department wants."

"ARAMCO has the oil concession with the Saudi government, not the U.S. government. The Saudis don't want U.S. government interference in Saudi Arabia, so the Saudi government listens to ARAMCO more than they listen to the State Department." George snorted. "I'm sure that irritates the State Department people to no end."

There was silence for a time, then George said softly, "I understand your dismay at the suffering these religions have caused over the centuries. You only need to live in this part of the world for a while to see how ridiculous it is that Jews and Moslems and Christians would fight each other over what is fundamentally the same religion. But never try to tell that to anyone, it just makes people mad."

She heard him settle into his sheets.

"I'm not really a deep believer," he continued. She was surprised at this candid monologue, masked by the darkness and quiet of the room. "But the funny thing is, I would still like for us to go to church when we move back to the States. Not every week, but sometimes. It is soothing."

Ruth wondered what effect George's father's suicide had had on his bright and sensitive only child. But she put that dark thought out of her mind and soon was sleeping.

Damascus was a pleasant sun-washed city, flowers everywhere. They had done some sightseeing the afternoon they arrived, then retired to the Vendome Hotel. The next morning they were pleased by the French-style breakfast served to them in a sunny courtyard.

"I'm really pleased that Mike is such a good traveler," Ruth said, sipping delicious espresso. "He seems to be enjoying himself no matter where we are, even riding hour after hour on the old MATS C-47s."

George smiled and pulled Michael back up into his chair. "What are you doing under the table?"

"I'm a squirrel," Michael said. Ruth handed him his iron skunk toy and he moved it around the linen tablecloth. The waiters' faces remained impassive.

They thanked the waiters and made their way down the red carpeted hallway to their suite of rooms on the second floor of the Vendome Hotel. "Damascus was the seat of Arab learning while Europe was still in the dark ages. Take astronomy for example, half the stars have Arabic names—Algol, Altair, Betelgeuse, Spica. They invented steel, Damascene steel for weapons. Medicine and basic hygiene. The Omayyad caliphs of the seventh century. Then later when the Abbasid caliphs…"

"What is a caliph anyway?" Ruth finally interrupted the stream of words.

"Leader of Islam. The Omayyads claimed to be descendants of Omar, the Abbasids were descendents of Abbas, both supposedly distant relatives of the prophet. Anyway, the Abbasid caliphs moved the capital of the Islamic world from Damascus to somewhere and then to Baghdad, and a golden age of education and culture began in the Arabic speaking world. About the year eight hundred the caliph was named Harun al-Rashid…" George looked expectantly at Ruth.

"The Arabian nights."

"Right. Literature about djinns and flying carpets, but also art and science. A hundred years before the Viking culture began spreading west across the Atlantic from Norway. Mainland Europe was sinking into the dark ages. Roman law was gone, the Catholics were still consolidating their empire. It was tribal, not even feudal—no culture, no art, no learning, no exploration. Nothing."

"You sound bitter," Ruth said.

"All those centuries lost," George said. "Think where we could be if Europeans hadn't wasted all those years."

"But now Arab culture is less advanced than European culture. How did they lose all that they had?"

"Wars," George said. "Islam became much the same as the Catholic Church in Europe in the Middle Ages. And for any political entity like that, change is bad." Ruth could see the controlled anger he'd had in him ever since he'd come back from his duty assignment in Europe in the closing days of World War Two. "Part of the change in Islam was caused by the Christians, the Crusaders, the European invaders." Ruth liked his eloquence, although he did go on a bit too long sometimes. But she was glad to see that being in lecture mode seemed to help him relax a bit.

Two hours from Damascus, the driver took them up the stony road to the citadel, a great white stone castle outside the city of Aleppo.

George read from the guide book he'd bought in Damascus. "This is a crusader castle. Two hundred years of fighting over who would control Jerusalem. Saladin finally broke the power of the Christian invaders about year twelve hundred." They walked for an hour over the gigantic structure, along the tops of battlements forty feet thick, around stone buildings now fallen into ruin. But the huge arched entrance still stood.

"I've moved some big stones out in the pasture back on the

farm," George told Ruth as they made their way back to the car. "I cannot imagine the effort it took to assemble this much rock on top of this hill."

"Decades of slave labor."

They rode in silence across the desert back toward Damascus. George sat staring in reflective silence. "Maybe we've immersed ourselves enough in biblical history..." Ruth said.

She patted his shoulder.

They were back in Damascus by nightfall and fell into bed exhausted.

"You've been here four months now," George said to Ruth as they sat in their comfortable living room after dinner at the officers' club. "Base housing, military supply, Air Force towels, sheets, blankets, plates. Riding the old C-47s. No department stores, no phones..."

"I don't mind base housing," Ruth said. "And this base is better than any of the Army bases where we lived in the States. Here there's less of the military..."

"Crap," George filled in for her. "The mindless drills, the rigid social hierarchy, all that stuff. We are here to operate an airfield and train the Saudis, both good things to do."

"I'm very proud of what you do," Ruth said quietly. "I'm proud of you."

A smile spread over George's face. "Thanks." He put his arms around her. "We've come a long way, haven't we? We've seen a lot already, and there's still so much more to see. I'm glad you like to travel."

"Michael too." Ruth smiled again and the same smile came to

George's face.

"He is a good traveler, isn't he? We're lucky." George smiled indulgently at Michael playing on the Persian carpet with his trucks and cars. Ever since their days of teaching at Ruhl School, George had been a polished public speaker. But sometimes, like now, the choreographed words and phrases dropped away and Ruth saw the bright, inquiring man inside the confident exterior. Ruth liked these occasional glimpses of the intelligent, but very private man she'd married.

The next weekend they went on another picnic with the James family. This time they went inland to where a village had once stood. They walked the sand, looking for coins and bits of pottery near a grove of date palms being choked with sand. They found a number of bits of metal that might have been coins.   After a while they took refuge from the heat under a palm tree.

"There's brackish water and some artesian wells here and there throughout this area," Vince told them. "That's why these villages are here in the first place. The bedouin learned to irrigate to grow date palms and forage for sheep, but with standing water came mosquitoes. ARAMCO just completed a four year program to eliminate anopheles mosquitoes and malaria all through this area."

Ruth and George exchanged looks. "The more I hear about

ARAMCO, the better I like it," George said.

"Maybe you should come to work for ARAMCO," Vince said.

"Maybe I should," he replied thoughtfully.

"I've got to make a trip back to Bangkok," George told Ruth one evening. "Just two days. There and back. Will you be OK here by yourself?"

Ruth gave him a hug. "Of course. I'm settled in. I even went to Khobar by myself the other day, rode the Air Force bus, just Michael and me. That's where I bought this set of drinking glasses." She held up one of the water glasses. It had a silver rim and the Saudi flag embossed on the side. George realized he'd seen them on the dinner table, but hadn't thought anything about them.

Ruth chuckled. "You should see your expression. Anyway, yes, I'll be fine here. Besides, it's not like I'm alone. This is a community here, a small town in the best sense, we all help each other."

Ruth enjoyed the next two days. As much as she loved George, it was good to have time to herself too.

Michael's third birthday was coming up and Ruth had arranged a birthday party for him. "I invited all the kids on base," George told Ruth. He eased into his chair and took Michael on his lap. "I expect we'll get eight, maybe ten."

Ruth smiled. "And I've got all the ingredients for the cake. Had to borrow candles and vanilla from Roz, but I'll bake it tonight and by lunchtime tomorrow it will be ready."

George smiled at Michael. "You're nearly three years old and already a world traveler. What do you think of that?"

"Good," Michael said firmly.

"I agree."

The next afternoon all the Air Force mothers brought their kids to the apartment dressed in their best, and probably only, party clothes. They played outside until the wind got too strong, then came inside and racketed around through the apartment. Paper plates, balloons,

and paper cups were strewn everywhere, the gifts forgotten as the kids ran and played in high spirits while the mothers huddled in the kitchen.

"Well," Roz said slowly, "it's nearly three. I'd better collect Robert and be going." In the living room the kids were falling into repose, beginning to play with the ubiquitous wooden blocks, dolls, and toy cars. Mothers collected their kids and soon the apartment was quiet. Ruth collected Michael from the couch. "I want to brush your teeth, then you need to take a nap before your father gets home."

A few minutes later, the sugar removed from his teeth, Michael climbed into his bed and began to drowse.

"Did you enjoy your birthday party?" Ruth asked as she tucked him in.

"It was the best one ever."

Ruth laughed and retreated to the living room to begin cleaning up.

When George got home she told him, "Michael said his birthday party today was the best one he'd ever had." They both laughed.

"Since he can't possibly remember the other two, I'd say that was a safe bet," George said. They laughed again. "But I like that optimistic attitude—each day is the best yet."

"A lot like you, I think," Ruth said. "Although I know you worry about your mother, alone on the farm. But she has neighbors and friends helping. It's a community there, just like it is here. She'll be fine. Her letters seem to say she is."

He nodded. "Yes."

But Ruth knew in her heart that all people feel loneliness when they live alone.

Chapter 12

In Baghdad, after a pleasant breakfast in the Zia Hotel dining room overlooking the Tigris River, the front desk staff informed them their guide was waiting for them. They introduced themselves to the guide, got into an old but well-maintained DeSoto, and set off for the ruins of the ancient cities to the south. Ruth carried her trusty black and red handbag and a thermos of drinking water. After an hour on the Basra highway they turned onto a rougher road and soon reached the site of ancient Babylon. They got out of the car into desert heat and unbroken silence. George wandered alone up the great staircases and down the ruined colonnades. Images of men three thousand years dead rose up in his imagination. He remembered sitting on the bench overlooking the Missouri River at St. Benedict's, his imagination on fire with the sights and sounds of ancient lands. George stood still in the shade of a ruined wall. He was here. The wall was dusty and rough under his fingers. He

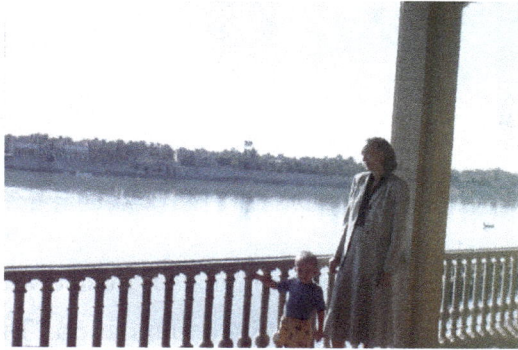

199

was here.

"I can imagine it all." George was more excited than Ruth had ever seen him. "Ur of the Chaldees, Babylon, Hammurabi's Code—the first laws ever written down. Ur was supposedly where Abraham of the bible came from. The Hittite empire, the Assyrians, those winged bull statues; did you see them?" George pointed past the walls."Not yet, George, slow down. This stuff has been here for three thousand years," she told him. "It'll wait another ten minutes."

"I want to get a picture of you and Michael. Abdullah, take to that place." He pointed to the next building foundation, lower than the one they stood on. "Picture."

Ruth followed the guide down one set of steps dusted with sand and up the next one to the top of the ruined foundation."This is where Sargon of Akkad once reigned," George shouted over to them.

Ruth smiled apologetically at the guide. "He is happy to be here."

"There is much to

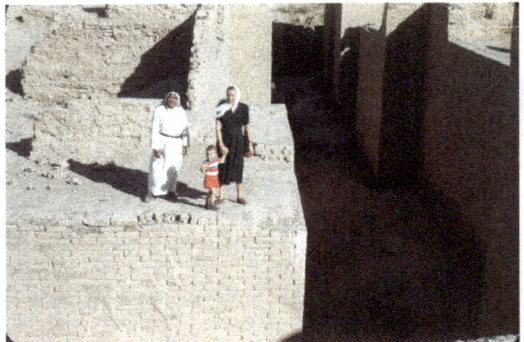

see," Abdullah said. Ruth and Michael followed the guide through the massive silent ruins. The desert stretched all around them, unchanged over millennia.

They eventually caught up with George getting a photo of a ziggurat. "Down near Basra is the fabled Garden of Eden, in the marshes at the confluence of the Tigris and Euphrates rivers."

"I think this will be enough for this trip," Ruth said. "I think we should drive back to Baghdad this afternoon."

George scurried off to get another picture.

The weather cooled somewhat as winter progressed. One day there were even a few clouds in the sky, but never rain.

On Christmas Eve George put on his class B uniform. Ruth put on the only dressy clothes she had—a skirt and a white linen blouse, with her ever-present loafers and bobby socks. They walked down the edge of the asphalt street to the O'Keefe's house in the calm desert evening. The day was warm, but not hot. "I love this kind of weather," Ruth said. "But not the humidity of summer nights."

"You sound like the ARAMCO guys," George said. "They're mostly from California."

"I kind of like it here," Ruth said, taking George's hand.

"I'm glad you do," he replied, gently disengaging his hand from hers. "But no public displays of affection, remember. Offensive to Saudi custom."

At the O'Keefe's there was a lavish buffet laid out, presided over by Luigi in a clean chef's uniform he'd wangled out of Air Force supplies. "Look at Dorothy Cretor's outfit!" Ruth whispered to

George. "Wristlets! I'm underdressed."

"You look fine," George reassured her. "After a while you will have seen every set of clothing every person here brought with them. That's the nice thing about uniforms, we're expected to look the same every day."

In the buffet line Ruth complimented Dorothy on her dress, which she seemed to expect. Roz O'Keefe laughed off Ruth's compliment on the food. "It's all Luigi's doing."

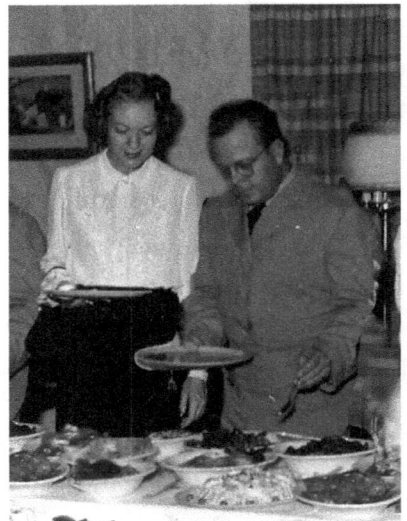

"I want to cook a big Christmas dinner when we're back in the States," Ruth told George. "On a snowy Christmas morning."

George hid his concern. "That's

a long way in the future, I'm afraid."

"But eventually."

He touched her hand. "Yes. And in the meantime I know you're worried about your father. But Bonnie is there to care for him and your mother."

Christmas morning Ruth woke Michael and the three of them sat in the quiet living room. Michael was puzzled by the packages, but willing to let his mother carefully unwrap his three presents one by one. "Can't easily get wrapping paper," George had told her, so she kept it neatly folded away in the closet, ready for the next gift.

They walked to the officers' club where there was a lightly attended brunch. After one cup of coffee, they said their farewells. "We're going to the field so Mike can see Santa arrive."

Santa arrived at noon on an Air Force C-47. When the plane had stopped and the door opened, Bill Charles emerged in a Santa suit and waved at the troop of kids and parents. A puzzled Michael stared as Santa walked by and got into an ARAMCO car for the drive up to the Dhahran compound.

"Let's walk to the bus stop," George suggested. "Santa will be up at the swimming pool for an hour, so we have plenty of time for

Mike to get his gift from Santa." He showed Ruth the small gift he had concealed in a MATS handbag for Santa to give to Michael.

Michael got his gift, then they sat on the sunny patio and ate cake and ice cream.

"It's nice up here," Ruth said. "The ARAMCO compound is nice."

They caught the ARAMCO bus back to the air base and walked down the road to their apartment. George carried Michael, who had fallen asleep after the cake and ice cream. When they stepped inside, the room that had seemed bright and festive that morning now felt gloomy. George clicked on the overhead light.

"That makes it worse," Ruth said. She turned on the table lamp Roz had loaned her. "Well…" she said. She laid Michael in his cot in the bedroom, settled down on the couch, and slipped her loafers off.

"I have one more Christmas gift for you," George said.

She eyed him. There were no hiding places in the house. She knew every cabinet and closet in the apartment, and there was nothing hidden away.

He stepped outside. "Open the door for me in a minute." When she did, he proudly brought in a small coffee table made of reddish wood, aromatic with fresh lacquer. He set it by the window.

"It's wonderful," Ruth breathed. "Where did you buy it?" She gave him a hug and kiss, then got the table runner and coffee pot they'd bought in Khobar and set them on the table.

"I had Enzo make it in the woodworking shop. He's a terrific woodworker, a real craftsmen. They're always asking me for something to do. Beats just sitting playing cards and waiting for their transport back to Italy."

"So much of their lives wasted," Ruth said. "The war's been over for four years."

"They don't complain. They like working for us. We pay them. Back in Italy their economy is a shambles. They live better here than they will there. They were drafted to fight Il Duce's war. Reestablish the Roman Empire."

Ruth put her hand over George's mouth. "Alright, alright, you're not back in the classroom teaching history. They are doing OK here, but I'm sure they still miss their families."

"By the way," George changed subjects, "how about a trip to Ethiopia? O'Keefe still hasn't banned taking families on the military attaché plane so..."

Ruth shushed him. "It all sounds good, but let's talk about it tomorrow. I'm tired."

The light coming in from the desert sunset was a buttery gold. Ruth moved the table over near the Persian carpet. George opened the door and the evening air came into the room like silent magic.

"Home," Ruth said.

George wisely said nothing.

"Michael's doing fine here," Ruth mused. "The other kids are nice. But he'll be old enough to start kindergarten next year."

"We're working on arrangements with ARAMCO to allow air base kids to go to school there," George told her.

Ruth got up and moved the new table slightly. "I like the table. Thank you."

George stood and put his arms around her. "Don't worry. We have another year until Michael needs to start kindergarten. We'll work something out."

"I know we will." She kissed him and pulled away gently. "But now I'm ready for bed."

February 7, 1950, Ruth and Michael and George boarded the C-47 for Ethiopia. The winter dawn was almost cool. The two hour flight to Jiddah was uneventful, the desert sunrise beautiful. On the ground, they refueled and were soon back in the air crossing the Red Sea.

"It's dark blue," Ruth commented. "I surprised at how dark it looks."

"It's deep, very deep, a rift in the earth," George said, craning to see more. "Same rift in the earth's surface that forms the Great Rift Valley in East Africa. We'll…"

"I know," Ruth said. "We'll go there one day."

It was late afternoon by the time the plane touched down at the tiny Asmara airport. There was a consulate car parked just beyond the fence. "Major Trial?"

George greeted the American sergeant driving and helped him load embassy mail and supplies. Then the car dropped them at the Ciaao Hotel.

"Pick you up at eight," the kid said and sped off. The Italian staff showed them their room and they settled in. Their room was large, comfortable, and had a nice balcony overlooking the street in front of the hotel.

The next day while George was inspecting a local school, Ruth and Michael strolled down the quiet empty street. The sun was warm and the air was filled with the pale scent of mud brick and dusty high-country foliage. At that moment it stuck her how far from home she was. The other side of the world from Kansas City. She felt fully in touch with the world, at ease travelling everywhere and anywhere.

A local woman carrying an infant in a white cloth passed her. They smiled at each other. Ruth walked on, then turned and watched the woman walk away, intent on her daily tasks. We live in cultures so different as to be incomprehensible to each other, Ruth thought. But we are both just people, raising kids, going about our lives. She stood watching the woman until she turned a corner and disappeared from sight.

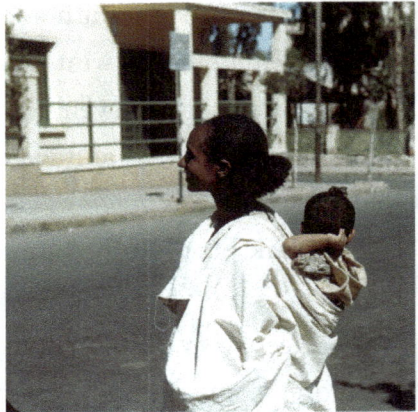

The next day they flew over dry upland country to Addis Ababa, the capital city. "A Christian country since antiquity. Emperor Haile Selassie is back on the throne since the end of the war, but lots of Italians are still here, our hotel manager for example."

In Addis Ababa, the American Consulate car picked them up along with the consulate mail and drove them to their hotel. "The Ras Hotel." Ruth smiled.

George toured a school, then the three of them shopped the street vendors for souvenirs. Always ready to document the next event, George took a photo of Michael in a donkey cart. The next morning they had the dining room to themselves for breakfast.

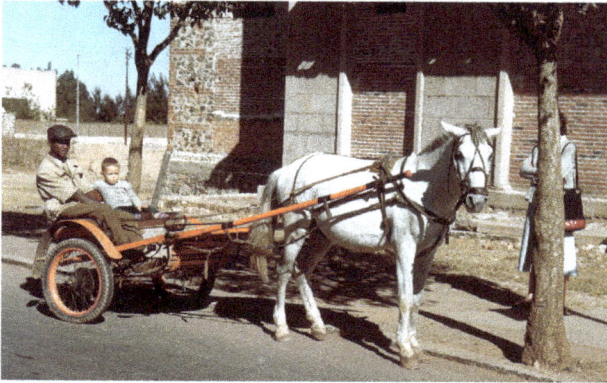

"You seem different these days," George told Ruth over breakfast. "How so?"

"More relaxed, more confident, happier."

She laid her hand over his on the white tablecloth. "I'm happier than I've ever been before."

"Even this far away from home?"

"Far away, but not from home." She smiled at him. "And I love to travel, with you and Michael. We've seen a lot already…"

"…and much more to come," George said. "We're lucky, aren't we?"

They had not been back at the air base a week when George broke the news to Ruth that he needed to go back to Bangkok. "The American Consulate there has made arrangements for me to tour a school and talk with the headmaster." He paused. "I'd like for you and Michael to go along."

209

Ruth nodded. "We've only been back from Ethiopia a week and you're ready to go again?"

"Thailand, the temples, the flowers…"

"I know, I know. Yes, we'll go. Of course we'll go."

The Persian carpet, the brass they'd bought, Michael's Arab clothing, the photos George had taken on their trips—their special belongings had transformed the small apartment into their home. Michael played contentedly on the floor with some wooden blocks the Italians had made in the wood shop.

"I've been at this air base for two full years now. You and Michael have been here for a year." He went to the door, opened it, and stood staring at the single paved street, the bougainvillea bushes, the date palms by the theater building.

Ruth recognized that long stare, and his frown of dissatisfaction. "How many Saudi students have been through your classes?"

"Over four hundred, but only a dozen have taken advantage of the overseas training I went to so much trouble to organize." He shrugged. "But I think Sessums and Snyder and I, we've accomplished something."

"Yes you have. I remember how proud you were when the first group graduated," Ruth said.

"Harry's leaving," George said suddenly.

Ruth frowned. "I'll miss Mildred, and Harry. Where's their new assignment? Washington?"

George averted her gaze. "No. It's just up the hill from here. Harry took a job with ARAMCO, in their training department."

Ruth brightened. "Right up the hill. We can still get together. Harry will be working for Vince James then?"

George closed the door and sat down. "Yes."

Ruth poured their coffee cups full. "Maybe that's what you should do too?"

He nodded. "Maybe so. You said yourself how nice the Dhahran compound seemed when we were there at Christmas time."

"Would you lose your Army time?" Ruth sat down slowly. "You went into the Army in September 1940, so you've got less than ten years…"

"Harry says the Air Force personnel guy at the military air assistance group in Jiddah told him he can stay in the active reserve, no break in service. He'll come back down here to the air base once a month for a day to stay active."

They heard Michael stirring in the other room. George went to the bedroom door and looked in for a moment, then went and opened the front door again and stood staring down the street toward the desert stretched out before him. Ruth knew that look. She'd seen it on his face when he was planning their trips to the ancient cities in Iraq, to Beirut, to Damascus, to the citadel at Aleppo, and to the Taj Mahal in India.

"Living in the ARAMCO compound would be fine with me," she said.

He smiled at her. "ARAMCO is doing the same thing we are, but they are doing it on a much bigger scale. It's a long term effort up there. Down here it's all temporary, focused on air base operations."

"The Thailand trip will take your mind off your worries here,"

Ruth reassured him. She also had something else to tell him, but now was not the moment. Not when he was distracted with worry about his training program and whether he should go to work for ARAMCO.

Bangkok was beautiful, relaxed, and exotic. They toured the floating market, took a river boat past the Temple of Dawn, and visited the temple of the Emerald Buddha. That evening at the hotel they had a wonderful dinner of lobster and shrimp.

Ruth waited until the dessert was served—some sort of rice pudding with what looked like gold foil on top. "I have something to tell you," she said as they sipped their coffee. She could tell by the expression on George's face that he was not happy with the taste of the coffee. She smiled. "We've been spoiled by fresh Arabian coffee."

"What was it you wanted to tell me?"

"I'm pregnant."

There was silence. Michael looked from his father's face to his mother's face, puzzled by the emotions he saw and the silence that had fallen between them.

George took Ruth's hands in his. "That's wonderful, when is the baby due?"

"June. Roz and I went up to the ARAMCO clinic last week."

The next morning George departed with two men from the American Embassy and a translator. Ruth and Michael had a leisurely breakfast, then strolled the hotel gardens. After a time the sun was getting hot so they returned to the hotel veranda for lemonade.

An American military car pulled up and George got out. He came up the front steps of the hotel, looking worried. Ruth's heart started pounding.

When he saw her, he stopped and took a deep breath. Then he walked over to her and put his arm around her.

"What's wrong? What is it?" she said.

They sat down together on the wicker couch. "There was a telegram at the embassy." He reached in his shirt pocket and pulled out a folded paper.

"The air base received a telex yesterday and sent one to the embassy here. Captain Sims gave it to me just a few minutes ago. Your father died, on the seventeenth of March."

Ruth said nothing, felt nothing but a great silence in her mind. George hugged her. "Why don't you rest for a while." He walked with her and Michael to their room, then went off to arrange for them to get on the next air attaché flight back.

Michael played contentedly on the floor with his toy truck.

Ruth drifted between sleep and waking. She felt no sadness, not yet. Her mind drifted as it had when she was a girl. Her mother and sister had always called her a dreamer, and maybe a little unsure of herself. But during this last year she had gained self-confidence. She knew how to travel now, without fear. And Michael had absorbed that fearlessness from her. They both loved the sound and the scent of the old C-47s they'd flown so many hours in, taking them to new and interesting places.

She dreamed of the sunny summer days when she'd helped her mother in the garden at the house on Central Avenue in Nevada.

One day, in the distant future, she would have a garden of her own.

She came awake feeling the pleasantly humid air of Thailand, kissed with the scent of frangipani. She remembered the silence of the temples they'd seen here in Bangkok, the soft patter of the monks' bare feet on polished tile floors, the immobile alien faces of the temple guardians and the Buddhas.

In a year of travelling, Ruth had learned that many tensions are left behind when we are far from home, and here on the other side of the world she felt perfectly at ease. Despite her father's death she felt calm and without sorrow. The dread of his impending death was gone now.

And wherever she was, she had George and Michael and the baby stirring inside her. She knew she had her family.

The flight would not depart until noon so the next morning Ruth asked George if they could make one more visit to a nearby

Buddhist temple. While Michael and George waited outside, she stepped inside. It was comfortably cool, scented with incense smoke from the bundles burning at either side of the room. The Buddha looked down at her with eyes enlightened and incomprehensible. Ruth folded her hands as she'd seen the monks do. A tear fell from her eye. She saw her father as he had been, back in Nevada. She remembered his encouraging words to her when she'd left for the University. And she saw him again, tending baby Michael, or sitting in his rocking chair in the sun on the back porch of the house in Kansas City. She remembered the calm expression on his face as he'd stood on the back porch the day she'd said goodbye to him.

She took a handkerchief out and dried her eyes. Incense smoke spiraled up silently to the intricately inlaid ceiling. Ruth bowed her head. "I hope my father was happy, most of the time. I think he was. I will believe he was."

She paused for a moment. "And…thank you, for everything I've been given." Then she dried her eyes and went back out into the sunshine.

When they returned to the air base, friends came by commiserating and trying to be helpful, but Ruth's mind was on packing for the trip home and on the baby that would arrive soon.

Two days later, in the cool desert dawn, Ruth paused to wave goodbye to George, who was standing just where she'd seen him the evening she'd first arrived in Saudi Arabia. They blew a kiss to each other, then she went into the old C-47 and sat down beside Michael.

On June 21, 1950, a pleasant summer afternoon in Kansas City, Ruth gave birth to a daughter. "Just can't seem to ever leave good

old Menorah hospital," Bonnie had joked when she'd brought Ruth to the hospital. After the delivery, Ruth was taken to a bed in the recovery ward where Michael and Bonnie and her mother were waiting. They and the doctor stood at her bedside smiling as the nurse handed Ruth the tiny bundle of warmth.

"A beautiful baby girl," the doctor said. "No complications whatsoever for either of you. What will you name her?"

Ruth and George had talked about the baby's name before she'd left the air base, but Ruth had not discussed it with her family. She looked down at the baby's peaceful face.

"Her name is Linden."

Postscript

After Linden's birth, my family returned to Saudi Arabia where my father had taken a job with ARAMCO, the Dhahran-based oil company. We lived in Dhahran for several years, returned to Missouri for a few years, lived in Lebanon, and then Saudi Arabia again, before returning to Missouri to stay. But those years and those travels are another story for a future volume of reminiscence.

I decided to end this volume with the birth of my sister Linden.

www.ingramcontent.com/pod-product-compliance
Lightning Source LLC
Chambersburg PA
CBHW070154310326
41914CB00100B/1904/J